The Canonical Function of Acts

The Canonical Function of Acts
A Comparative Analysis

David E. Smith

A Michael Glazier Book

THE LITURGICAL PRESS
Collegeville, Minnesota

www.litpress.org

A Michael Glazier Book published by The Liturgical Press.

Cover design by David Manahan, O.S.B. Illustration detail: Map of the voyages of Peter and Paul from *Sacra Bibbia di Vence*, 1835.

1   2   3   4   5   6   7   8   9

Library of Congress Cataloging-in-Publication Data

Smith, David E., 1963–
    The canonical function of Acts : a comparative analysis / David E. Smith
        p. cm.
    "A Michael Glazier book."
    Includes bibliographical references and index.
    ISBN 0-8146-5103-8 (alk. paper)
    1. Bible. N.T. Acts—Criticism, interpretation, etc. 2. Bible. N.T.—Canon.
I. Title.

BS2625.2 .S63 2002
226.6'012—dc21

                                                    2001038824

To my wonderful wife,
Patricia A. Smith,
whose loving and faithful support made this research possible,
and to the Rev. Jonathan E. Barr,
friend and theological conversation partner,
this book is gratefully dedicated.

Contents

Illustrations

Abstract

The New Testament book of Acts was recognized as canonical throughout most of the catholic Christian world by the early third century of the common era. Although the association of its author with the apostle Paul gave the text *a priori* authority, it was the content of Acts that finally caused it to achieve canonical status. By linking the Old Testament with the ministries of Jesus, the Jerusalem apostles, Paul, and the "bishops" of Ephesus by means of its pneumatology, Acts could function both as a unifier of the developing canon and as a justification for the hermeneutical authority of the catholic bishops. This is the twofold canonical function of Acts.

The function of Acts as unifier of the developing biblical canon was established in the late second and early third centuries in the context of the catholic-Gnostic disputes over Scripture, and it became a part of the Church's perpetual understanding of Acts. By the late fourth century, the use of Acts to legitimize the hermeneutical claims of the catholic bishops began to rival its use as a canonical unifier. In this way Acts aided the developing catholic network of churches in their appropriation of the entire biblical canon as a collection of witnesses to trinitarian theology.

An analysis of the apocryphal Acts demonstrates an alternative understanding of religious authority on the part of their authors, one which seemed to undermine the catholic approach to Scripture. The canonization of the Lukan Acts precluded the canonization of other Acts and partially explains how a collection of diverse texts was accepted and promoted in the Church as a unified corpus.

Introduction

Approximately 1,900 years after the last New Testament document was written, the subject of the New Testament canon remains a prime subject of scholarly inquiry. In recent years we have seen something of a resurgence in canon scholarship. This is due in part to the questions raised by the results of historical criticism, the discovery of many non-canonical Jewish and Christian writings of antiquity, new studies on the development of the Hebrew canon, Septuagintal studies, greater awareness of early Christian conflicts, the convictions of many scholars that the New Testament writings themselves show remarkable diversity, and modern ecumenical discussions.[1]

Definitions

The English word "canon" is derived from the Greek word *kanōn*, which in its literal sense means a rod or rule used to measure or guide.[2] Metaphorically, *kanōn* signifies a standard—something by which other things can be measured. In antiquity, the word was used to identify appropriate standards in a variety of contexts, including art, music, literature, ethics, law, and philosophy.[3] But *kanōn* also came to signify a list,

---

[1] See the discussion in Harry Y. Gamble, *The New Testament Canon: Its Making and Meaning* (Philadelphia: Fortress Press, 1985) 13–14. For a history of modern New Testament canon scholarship, see Bruce M. Metzger, *The Canon of the New Testament: Its Origin, Development, and Significance* (New York: Oxford University Press, 1987) 11–36.

[2] Liddell and Scott, *An Intermediate Greek-English Lexicon* (Oxford: Oxford University Press, 1994 reprint) 399.

[3] Gamble, *NT Canon*, 15. For a helpful overview of the Hellenistic background of the word "canon" and its use in early Christianity, see Eric F. Osborn, "Reason and

because of the markings on the measuring rod. Both of these metaphorical meanings are implied in the word "canon" as it is applied to the collection of authoritative Christian texts.[4] Therefore, as a basis for its use throughout this work, canon is defined broadly here as *a collection of religiously authoritative texts*.[5] This is what I call the lexical definition and it is useful because it is narrow enough to identify the two key concepts involved in the phenomenon of the biblical canon (namely, the collective and authoritative elements) and yet broad enough to account for different nuances detectable in the use of the word "canon" and in the form and function of the canon evident in different times and places throughout the history of the Church.[6] Beyond this broad lexical definition of canon, however, it is necessary to explicate the concept of authority in connection with the canon. In what sense (or senses) was the canon authoritative for the early Church? Do all the texts of Scripture function in the same way as authoritative documents? The lexical definition offered above and operative throughout this project is the conceptual definition of canon. Beyond this, I offer the following functional definitions of the Christian canon in order to further define the concept of authority implicit in the notion of canon:

---

the Rule of Faith in the Second Century AD," *The Making of Orthodoxy,* ed. R. Williams (Cambridge: Cambridge University Press, 1989) 40–61.

[4] For a linguistic discussion of *kanōn,* including its possible semitic roots, see Gamble, *NT Canon,* 15–18. Cf. Ron Grove, "Canon and Community: Authority in the History of Religions" (Ph.D. diss., University of California, Santa Barbara, 1983), a work devoted almost exclusively to the definition of "canon."

[5] It is important to note that canon is not defined here as a collection of *authoritative religious texts.* It would appear that books like Esther and the Song of Solomon are not in and of themselves religious writings; neither one even refers to God. But these works have become in some sense religiously authoritative by their placement in a religious literary canon and by the application of a theological hermeneutic whereby God is read into the story and the text is made applicable to the religious life of the community, as in the reading of the Song as an expression of Christ's relationship to the Church.

[6] A prime example of this difference is the issue of canonical boundaries. Are the boundaries of the canon clearly and absolutely identifiable? For some groups of Christians the answer is a self-evident yes—for them the final form of the canon is the unquestioned point of departure for the study of Christian belief and practice. However, differences in the makeup of the canon evident throughout the history of the Church, including but not limited to the inclusion of the Old Testament Apocrypha, demonstrate the Church's inability to define the precise boundaries of the canon. The definition proposed here accounts for the two key characteristics of the canon and also allows for difference in the precise makeup of its contents.

1. Canon is the primary witness to the community's revelatory claims. This is the theological definition.[7]

2. Canon is the primary textual basis for public reading and proclamation. This is the liturgical definition.

3. Canon is the boundaries of orthodoxy and the textual basis for the authority of community leaders. This is the ecclesiastical definition.

4. Canon is the primary textual "holy of holies" where the believer experiences God. This is the devotional definition.

5. Canon is a primary tangible representation of divine transcendence. This is the psychological definition.[8]

6. Canon is the primary early documentation of the community's basic worldview. This is the historical definition.

7. Canon is the primary textual construction of communal identity. This is the sociological definition.[9]

These definitions encompass the specific functional aspects of the authority of the canonical documents in the life of the community. Furthermore, I would suggest that different texts within the canon function in these various ways to a greater or lesser extent depending on both the nature of the particular text and the historical context of its use. That is, while all the texts are implicitly authoritative by virtue of the canonical recognition given to them by the community, they function as authoritative documents in different ways based upon both intrinsic and extrinsic factors. For example, the psalms in general carry a certain implicit devotional and liturgical authority due to their nature, content, and use in worship. But specific psalms also contain theological authority for the Church because of the traditional messianic readings given to them by Christians throughout the centuries. A classic example is Psalm 110:1, which declares, "The LORD says to my lord,

---

[7] This theological definition is useful, in my view, because it allows for the number of different theological definitions and descriptions which have been offered by Christians throughout the history of the Church.

[8] The use of the indefinite article here is intentional. One could argue, for example, that icons are as much or more of a tangible representation of divine transcendence in Eastern Orthodoxy than is Scripture.

[9] This sociological definition is based primarily on the works of James Sanders. See, for example, his *Canon and Community: A Guide to Canonical Criticism* (Philadelphia: Fortress Press, 1984) 25, 33.

'Sit at my right hand until I make your enemies your footstool.'"[10] This text has traditionally been a key Old Testament text for the Church's christology. Jesus himself is quoted by the gospel writers as having used the text messianically (Matt 22:43-44; Mark 12:35-36; Luke 20:41-43). Furthermore, the lectionaries of the Church (both ancient and modern) obviously set apart certain texts as liturgically authoritative for those who use the lectionaries. Again, certain texts were used more centrally than others in particular polemical disputes during the early centuries of the Church's history. For example, during the Arian controversy the Alexandrians and their post-Nicene supporters used the texts of John 1 and Hebrews 1 frequently to defend their views, while the Arians used, among others, the text of Proverbs 8 and particular New Testament passages that emphasized the development of the character of Jesus.

Examples of this sort could be multiplied. The point here is that the specific manifestations of biblical authority in the early Church (and even in the present day) depend upon both the character of the text in question and the particular historical or social context in which the text is being used.[11] With regard to the argument that I make for Acts below, it will become clear as the project progresses that the primary functional definition of canon that operates for Acts in the writings of the Church Fathers is, in my view, the ecclesiastical one. That is, the primary value that Acts had for those who canonized it was directly related to the structure of canonical and ecclesiastical authority.

The Place of Acts in the Canon

In this project I want to examine the specific role that Acts played in the development of early catholicism in general and the New Testament canonical process in particular. I refer to this role as the *canonical function* of Acts. Why was Acts included in the catholic canon? What

[10] Unless otherwise indicated, all biblical quotations in this project are taken from *The HarperCollins Study Bible: New Revised Standard Version* (New York: Harper-Collins, 1993). Quotations from the NIV are taken from *The Holy Bible: New International Version* (Grand Rapids, Mich.: Zondervan, 1978). Those taken from the NKJV are from *The Holy Bible Containing the Old and New Testaments: The New King James Version* (Nashville: Thomas Nelson Publishers, 1983).

[11] The focus of this project is on the development and function of the canon in the early Church, but the principles expounded here with regard to the functional authority of Scripture continue to manifest themselves even today. For example, the liturgical authority of the Bible is relativized by those churches today which choose not to follow the injunction of Jesus to anoint the head when fasting (Matt 6:17) or that of Paul to greet one another with a holy kiss (1 Cor 16:20).

value did it hold for the Fathers who contributed to the formation of catholic thought and the catholic biblical canon? In the minds of the canonizers, how did Acts relate to other scriptural writings? The answers to these questions can only be found in the critical examination of both the text of Acts itself and the patristic use of Acts. It is my thesis that Acts functioned simultaneously for the Fathers as the unifier of the biblical canon and as a justification for the episcopal hermeneutical claim by means of its pneumatology. That is, Acts possessed great value for the bishops who claimed to be the successors of the apostles because it seemed to provide a basis for their claim that the entire biblical canon bore witness to their (developing) trinitarian theology. Acts provided this basis by linking the Old Testament texts with the teachings of Jesus, the Jerusalem apostles, and Paul, and by legitimizing a form of postapostolic authority—all by means of its pneumatology.

During the early twentieth century Harnack argued that Acts stood at the center of the New Testament canon, but his proposal was part of a theory of canon that is no longer tenable. He argued that the New Testament canon was, quite simply, a late-second-century C.E. creation that immediately took on a life of its own and superceded the "rule of faith" as the primary formulation of catholic belief. In support of this theory, Harnack maintained that Justin's *Dialogue with Trypho* and the Montanist movement provide strong testimony to the absence of a New Testament canon in the middle of the second century. Irenaeus, he argued, provides evidence of the existence of a "new collection of sacred books" around 185 C.E., and Tertullian and the Muratorian Canon are witnesses to the fact that by the year 200 the New Testament collection had become "closed and definite" in form.[12] Harnack argued that the New Testament canon was determined "simply [by] the Church of Rome" and that the various portions of the New Testament were "linked together by the central position of the Acts of the Apostles."[13] In his estimation, Acts "formed the bridge" between the Gospels and the Pauline epistles, and gave Paul legitimation by linking him with the Twelve.[14] Harnack even went so far as to claim that Luke laid the foundation for "that reverence for the Apostolic side by side with the Evangelic" from which arose the conception of apostolic tradition, and that without Acts "we should have had no New Testament."[15] That Harnack

[12] Adolf von Harnack, *The Origin of the New Testament*, trans. J. R. Wilkinson (New York: The Macmillan Co., 1925) 94–95.

[13] Ibid., 104.

[14] Ibid., 53, 64–68, 96.

[15] Adolf von Harnack, *The Acts of the Apostles*, trans. J. R. Wilkinson (New York: G. P. Putnam's Sons, 1909) 301.

clearly overstated this latter point is demonstrated by the existence within Marcionism of a canon of one gospel and ten epistles alone (without Acts).

A modified version of Harnack's canon history was presented by von Campenhausen. Most significantly, von Campenhausen argued with Harnack that "both the Old and the New Testaments had in essence already reached their final form and significance around the year 200."[16] In his view, the canon was created because of Marcionism, and restricted because of Montanism.[17] That is, Marcion forced the issue of the creation of a distinctively Christian literary canon, and the revelatory claims of the Montanists constrained the catholic officials to limit the canonical collection. For von Campenhausen, the late-second-century Muratorian Canon list—with its inclusion of the Gospels, Acts, Pauline epistles, two Johannine epistles, Jude, and Revelation—was evidence that the canon had been established by this time.[18]

This version of the development of the New Testament canon was challenged by Sundberg in his influential 1968 article on the history of the canon. Sundberg argued that the fourth century—rather than the second—was the century of "canonization." Sundberg makes a distinction between "Scripture" and "canon," arguing that the former is "religious literature that is appealed to for religious authority," while the latter represents a "closed collection of 'scripture,' to which nothing is to be added, from which nothing is to be subtracted."[19] Crucial to Sundberg's case is his redating of the Muratorian Canon list to the fourth century.[20] The implication of his work is that the use of Acts by the late-second- and early-third-century Fathers was not as significant for the formation of the canon as Harnack had imagined, a point seized upon and developed by Kuck who argues that Acts was not structurally significant for the Fathers in their construction of a literary canon.[21]

Sundberg's redating of the Muratorian Canon has been rejected by most scholars. Ferguson's rebuttal in 1982 has upheld the traditional

---

[16] Hans von Campenhausen, *The Formation of the Christian Bible,* trans. J. A. Baker (Philadelphia: Fortress Press, 1968/1972 translation) 327.

[17] Ibid., 163, 221.

[18] Ibid., 210–68. See below for a more complete discussion of the Muratorian Canon.

[19] A. C. Sundberg, Jr., "Toward a Revised History of the New Testament Canon," *Studia Evangelica* 4 (1968) 454.

[20] Ibid., 458; idem, "Canon Muratori: A Fourth-Century List," *Harvard Theological Review* 66/1 (January 1973) 1–41.

[21] David W. Kuck, "The Use and Canonization of Acts in the Early Church" (STM Thesis, Yale University, 1975).

dating of the canon within the field of early Christian studies.[22] Further-more, although it is true that the word "canon" is not used of Scripture before the fourth century, most scholars have rejected the formal distinction between "Scripture" and "canon" made by Sundberg. Childs is typical of this attitude when he argues that such a formal distinction distorts the reality of the canonical process by shifting the focus to the final stage.[23]

But Sundberg's work appears to have contributed to the change in the way canon history is now written. To bring the process of canonization to a virtual end around the year 200 as Harnack and von Campenhausen did is no longer tenable. As the magisterial work of Metzger demonstrates, the formation of the New Testament canon in the early Church is now seen by most scholars as a gradual process that took place between the second and fourth centuries, with a significant "growth spurt" at the end of the second century.[24]

In my estimation, Harnack's proposal that Acts performed a unifying function in the canon of the early Church suffered somewhat in late-twentieth-century scholarship because it was a part of a theory of canon formation that has been discredited.[25] For example, Haenchen argues that "only because of its connection with the third gospel . . . was Acts allowed to cross the threshold of the Canon."[26] Although he acknowledges that Acts had value for Irenaeus in demonstrating the unity of the apostolic message, he makes no connection between this phenomenon and the canonicity of Acts, apparently failing to account for intrinsic textual factors in the canonization of the New Testament documents.

Clearly there were significant problems with Harnack's proposal. His contention that the New Testament canon was a second-century creation fails to give adequate attention to developments in the third and fourth centuries. The role played by Rome in the formation of the canon was overemphasized by Harnack. His conviction that the four Gospels had been placed side by side as a collection in Asia Minor in

[22] E. Ferguson, "Canon Muratori: Date and Provenance," *Studia Patristica* 17 (1982) 677–82.

[23] Brevard S. Childs, *The New Testament as Canon: An Introduction* (Valley Forge, Pa.: Trinity Press International, 1985/1994 reprint) 238.

[24] Bruce M. Metzger, *The Canon of the New Testament: Its Origin, Development, and Significance* (Oxford: Oxford University Press, 1987).

[25] Bruce, however, in his scholarship, continued to uphold the notion that Acts links the Gospels and the Pauline epistles, giving credit to Harnack for the idea. See F. F. Bruce, *The Canon of Scripture* (Downers Grove: InterVarsity Press, 1988) 132–33.

[26] Ernst Haenchen, *The Acts of the Apostles: A Commentary* (Philadelphia: The Westminster Press, 1971) 9.

the early second century lacks sufficient evidence. And his perception of the relative independence of the New Testament from the broader stream of tradition betrays a Protestant bias. But his insight into the unifying function of Acts in the polemics of the late-second-century Fathers is not without merit. I want to propose an expanded and more carefully nuanced version of this part of Harnack's argument based upon the new model of canon history. I will argue that Acts not only linked the Gospels with the Pauline epistles in the judgment of the Fathers, but that it also linked those texts with the Old Testament and the catholic epistles, *and* it provided a basis for the catholics to claim the exclusive right of biblical interpretation vis-à-vis their opponents by its support of postapostolic ecclesiastical authority. Furthermore, I will argue that beginning in the fourth century a historical development is noticeable in regard to the issue of episcopal hermeneutical authority.

The Development of the New Testament Canon

What follows is an overview of the development of the New Testament canon from a historical perspective based upon patristic sources and a consensus of recent New Testament scholarship. This overview is not intended to be a comprehensive account of the catholic use of Scripture or of the disputes which contributed to the development of the canon. Rather, it is intended to be representative of the current scholarly (three-century) model of canon formation and is given: (1) in order to situate the project squarely within contemporary scholarly discourse; and (2) to provide the backdrop and foundation for what follows in this work. It has become clear that the New Testament canon came into existence as the result of a complex of historical circumstances and theological challenges which the catholic Church faced throughout the first four centuries of the common era.[27]

[27] Whenever the subject of a sacred literary canon is broached, it is imperative to ask the simple but often overlooked question, *whose* canon are we analyzing? It is with this question in mind that I repeatedly refer to the *catholic* Church and its doctrines, leaders, and sacred texts. I use the word "catholic" (meaning "universal") as a value-neutral term to describe the networks of churches around the Mediterranean that gradually developed into the forms recognizable to the contemporary person, namely the Eastern Orthodox and Roman Catholic/Protestant churches of later centuries, and which "canonized" the twenty-seven books of the New Testament. Catholicism was a method of organizing and answering religious questions to which some, but not all, Christians in the early centuries subscribed. This phenomenon is described by Koester as "Panchristianity," the establishment of formal relationships between churches that share a "common ritual and a common story" and which gradually evolved into the catholic Church proper. See Helmut Koester,

1. First Century

While few scholars would argue that the New Testament writings themselves predict or prescribe the idea or limits of a Christian literary canon, it does seem that the seeds of canonicity are found within some of these writings. Several concepts should be noted. First, the notion of apostolic authority, which was to become a monumental issue in the Church as it later developed, is clearly upheld in the New Testament documents themselves. For example, passages like Matthew 16:18 ("you are Peter, and on this rock I will build my church") and Ephesians 2:19-20 ("the household of God, built upon the foundation of the apostles and prophets") establish the primacy of the apostolic office and teaching. Second, the priority of believing and preserving apostolic tradition is also taught in several of the New Testament documents. For

---

"Writings and the Spirit: Authority and Politics in Ancient Christianity," *Harvard Theological Review* 84/4 (1991) 353–72. As Wall notes, "The catholicizing church was also the canonizing church, which formed the biblical canon in order to form the church catholic." See R. Wall and E. Lemcio, *The New Testament as Canon: A Reader in Canonical Criticism* (Sheffield: JSOT Press, 1992) 24. I have intentionally avoided the use of the term "orthodox" as a descriptive in this regard, for although the terms "catholic" and "orthodox" are sometimes used interchangeably in modern literature and discourse, they in fact imply quite different things. The former represents a method of thinking and organizing, while the latter represents a value judgment. Ehrman addresses the problem of categories and labels in pre-Nicene Christianity. After giving a nice overview of the history of the Christian conception of the categories "orthodox" and "heretical," he argues that these terms can be used as sociopolitical designations (apart from any theological value judgment) from the fourth century on, when one version of Christianity clearly gained power. But he asks the question whether these labels are accurate designations in any sense for pre-Nicene versions of Christianity. Since the Fathers of the fourth century and beyond claimed particular pre-Nicene figures as their forebears (including Ignatius, Polycarp, Justin, Irenaeus, Tertullian, Hippolytus, Clement, and Origen), Ehrman suggests the terms "proto-orthodox" to describe these persons (and others who shared their views) and "incipient orthodoxy" as a designation for their doctrines. However, because of the cumbersome nature of these terms he chooses to retain the traditional labels "orthodoxy" and "heresy" (and their counterparts) as value-neutral designations. In my judgment, the term "catholic" is the best choice to describe the networks of churches and persons who contributed to the gradual development of that form of Christianity which gained permanent prominence in the fourth century. Although it would be a mistake to think that even these shared a monolithic theology, with Ehrman I affirm that "there are certain points of continuity among these thinkers and clear lines of development that move toward the fourth century." See Bart D. Ehrman, *The Orthodox Corruption of Scripture: The Effect of Early Christological Controversies on the Text of the New Testament* (New York: Oxford University Press, 1993) 3–13.

example, in 1 Corinthians 11:2 Paul declares to the Corinthians, "I commend you because you remember me in everything and maintain the traditions just as I handed them on to you." Furthermore, the author of the Pastorals exhorts his readers to guard what had been entrusted to them, to avoid "the profane chatter and contradictions of what is falsely called knowledge," to guard "the good treasure" entrusted to them with the help of the Holy Spirit living in them, and to entrust to faithful people what they had heard from him so that they might be able to teach others as well (1 Tim 6:20; 2 Tim 1:14; 2:2).

And finally, it is essential to observe that the idea and authority of written tradition or revelation was present during the first century, even when oral tradition was so prevalent. For example, Paul (or a Pauline disciple) urges his readers to "stand firm and hold fast to the traditions that you were taught by us, either by word of mouth *or* by our letter" (2 Thess 2:15). The author of Revelation states, "Blessed is the one who reads aloud the words of the prophecy, and blessed are those who hear and who keep what is written in it; for the time is near" (Rev 1:3). He also issues the following warning:

> I warn everyone who hears the words of the prophecy of this book: if anyone adds to them, God will add to that person the plagues described in this book; if anyone takes away from the words of the book of this prophecy, God will take away that person's share in the tree of life and in the holy city, which are described in this book (Rev 22:18-19).

While not prescribing the precise notion or limits of a written canon, these sample New Testament references are sufficient to indicate that apostolic and/or divine authority had been attached to certain writings by their authors. And if the Church was to recognize and accept the authority of any of these, it would have to discriminate in some way between writings in order to decide which ones to accept as authoritative and which ones to reject.[28]

2. Late First and Early Second Centuries

One of the earliest noncanonical writings that has survived is the *First Epistle of Clement,* which most scholars have dated to the last decade of the first century. The epistle was written by Clement of Rome to the church at Corinth in regard to certain disputes which had arisen

---

[28] This is not to say that a literary canon was the only way for this concern to be addressed; merely that the issue of competing authoritative claims lies at the heart of the canon issue.

there.[29] Clement's primary authority is the Old Testament, which he quotes over one hundred times and in regard to which he uses the standard introductory formulas "the Scripture says" and "it is written."[30] He does, however, quote the words of Jesus twice. In paragraph thirteen Clement writes, "most of all remembering the words of Jesus which he spake, teaching forbearance and long-suffering," after which he quotes several statements which are also found in Matthew and Luke. But since the form and order of the statements do not come from either gospel, and because similar formulations are found in Polycarp and Clement of Alexandria, Metzger has suggested the possibility that Clement is here using a catechetical formula.[31] The second use of the words of Jesus found in Clement occurs in paragraph 46, where he again introduces the quotation with the words "remember the words of Jesus our Lord," after which he quotes several statements with close parallels in the Synoptics. However, at the beginning and the end of the quotation, Clement includes warnings against offending and perverting "one of Mine elect" which are not found in the canonical Gospels.

Clement's use of Paul is fairly clear. For example, in paragraph 47 he instructs the Corinthians to "take up the epistle of the blessed Paul the Apostle." Metzger has observed that Clement makes reference to First Corinthians, Romans, Galatians, Philippians, and Ephesians, and that he alludes repeatedly to Hebrews and possibly to Acts, James, and 1 Peter.[32] It seems, therefore, that while Clement uses the Old Testament as his scriptural authority, he also regards Jesus, Paul, and certain catholic epistle traditions (and possibly some catholic epistles themselves) as authoritative. Yet he never refers to a New Testament writing as "scripture."[33]

---

[29] J. B. Lightfoot and J. R. Harmer, eds., *The Apostolic Fathers: Revised Greek Texts with Introductions and English Translations* (Grand Rapids, Mich.: Baker Book House, 1984 reprint) 3. Unless otherwise noted, all quotations from the Apostolic Fathers are taken from this edition.

[30] Metzger, *The Canon,* 41. The designation "Old Testament" is used throughout this project in the context of early Christianity and is not meant as a value judgment on the writings contained in this collection. This seems appropriate to me when dealing with the Christian appropriation of the sacred writings of ancient Israel and Second Temple Judaism because that is the early Christian designation for this collection. It also avoids the confusion over the use of the Septuagint or other translations in the early Christian community. The phrase "Hebrew Bible" is used here when referring to the canon in a Jewish context or when the Hebrew "originals" are in view.

[31] Ibid., 41–42.

[32] Ibid., 42–43.

[33] Ibid.

A similar situation is found with Ignatius of Antioch (ca. 110 C.E.). While numerous gospel traditions found (especially) in Matthew and John are also found in the epistles of Ignatius, there are no direct quotations from any canonical Gospels nor are they referred to as "scripture."[34] And while Ignatius shows apparent familiarity with many of the Pauline writings (including Romans, 1 Corinthians, Ephesians, Philippians, Galatians, Colossians, and 1 Thessalonians) and possible knowledge of Hebrews and 1 Peter, there is no instance of his referring to any of them as "scripture" either.[35] The teachings about Jesus, however, were apparently of supreme authority for Ignatius. In the eighth paragraph of his *Letter to the Philadelphians*, he states, "my charter is Jesus Christ, the inviolable charter is His cross and His death and His resurrection, and faith through Him. . . ." McDonald has concluded, therefore, that for Ignatius, the authority of the event of Jesus and the early Christian kerygma about that event were even more authoritative than the Old Testament.[36]

The *Didache* (late first or early second century) is another witness to the state of the canon during the time of the Apostolic Fathers. In it we find numerous canonical gospel-like sayings woven into the fabric of the text, some of which are parallel to statements in Matthew.[37] And yet there is at least one apocryphal saying (of Jesus?) in the text. It is found in paragraph one, where the author states, "Yea, as touching this also it is said; Let thine alms sweat into thine hands, until thou shalt have learnt to whom to give." When the author refers to "the Gospel" (which he does several times) it is unclear whether this is a written document or a body of teaching ascribed to Jesus, but the latter seems more probable due to the generality and singularity of the references. The author refers to "the ordinance of the Gospel," the peace which is found "in the Gospel," and the necessary works prescribed "in the Gospel of our Lord" (11, 14). Metzger has concluded that for the author of the *Didache*, the ultimate authority for the Church is "the traditional teaching deriving from the Lord."[38]

Another early witness to the state of the canon in the early second century is Papias. Fragments of his works have survived through Eusebius, and these statements are very significant with regard to the developing New Testament canon. Besides giving direct witness to his

---

[34] Ibid., 45–48.

[35] Ibid., 49.

[36] Lee M. McDonald, *The Formation of the Christian Biblical Canon* (Nashville: Abingdon Press, 1988) 78.

[37] Compare paragraphs eight and nine with Matthew 6:9-13; 7:6.

[38] Metzger, *The Canon*, 51.

knowledge of the Gospel of Matthew (or proto-Matthew) and the Gospel of Mark, he also states his apparent preference for oral tradition over any written testimony when he states:

> [Whenever] anyone came, who had been a follower of the elders I questioned him in regard to the words of the elders—what Andrew or what Peter said, or what was said by Philip, or by Thomas, or by James, or by John, or by Matthew, or by any other of the disciples of the Lord, and what things Aristion and the presbyter John, the disciples of the Lord, say. For I did not think that what was to be gotten from the books would profit me as much as what came from the living and abiding voice (*E.H.* 3.39.1-4).[39]

Another statement of Papias (preserved in Eusebius) is significant for the study of the development of the New Testament canon in the early church. Regarding the Gospel of Mark he states,

> Mark, having become the interpreter of Peter, wrote down accurately, though not indeed in order, whatsoever he remembered of the things said or done by Christ. For he neither heard the Lord nor followed him, but afterward, as I said, he followed Peter, who adapted his teaching to the needs of his hearers, but with no intention of giving a connected account of the Lord's discourses, so that Mark committed no error while he thus wrote some things as he remembered them. For he was careful of one thing, not to omit any of the things which he had heard, and not to state any of them falsely (*E.H.* 3.39.15-16).

Gamble has noted that Papias' defense of Mark implies that the gospel had been the object of criticism, possibly in regard to its lack of chronological accuracy or its incompleteness.[40] To this list of possible early criticisms of Mark, Metzger adds the fact that Mark had not followed Jesus himself.[41] He has also concluded from scattered statements in antiquity that Papias knew of the Gospel of John, 1 Peter, 1 John, and Revelation, but that there is no surviving evidence that Papias knew of Luke or Paul.[42] It is unclear to what extent these texts functioned for him as authoritative documents.

---

[39] Unless otherwise noted, all quotations from the Church Fathers (except the Apostolic Fathers) are taken from the Eerdmans reprint edition; Greek terms are from Migne.

[40] Gamble, *NT Canon*, 26.

[41] Metzger, *The Canon*, 55.

[42] Ibid.

The *Epistle of Barnabas* is another witness to the state of the developing New Testament canon in this period. The author of this work quotes both the Old Testament and noncanonical Jewish writings as authoritative, even referring to the author of 2 Esdras as a "prophet" (12:1). And although Synoptic traditions can be found in the epistle (as well as themes possibly taken from 1 Timothy, 2 Timothy, and Revelation), there are no clear quotations from any New Testament writings, nor are any of them referred to as "scripture."[43] The word "gospel" is used by the author as a designation for the preaching of the apostles (5:9, 8:3).

Polycarp also represents a significant witness to the state and development of the canon in the early second century. In paragraph six of his *Letter to the Philippians,* he states: "Let us therefore so serve Him . . . as He himself gave commandment and the Apostles who preached the Gospel to us and the prophets who proclaimed beforehand the coming of our Lord. . . ." Based on this statement, Metzger has concluded that for Polycarp there existed a threefold hierarchy of authority. The teachings of Jesus *on their own* represented the highest level of authority, with the apostles second (as witnesses of Christ's words) and the prophets third (as those who predicted the coming of Christ).[44] This theory does find support in the fact that Polycarp feels no need to identify quotations of Jesus with written Gospels, as in his injunction to remember "the words which the Lord spake, as He taught: 'Judge not that ye be not judged' . . ." (*Epistle* 2:3). It is significant, however, that Polycarp appears to allude to Romans, 1 Corinthians, Galatians, Ephesians, Philippians, 2 Thessalonians, 1 Timothy, 2 Timothy, Hebrews, 1 Peter, and 1 John.[45] In paragraph 12, Polycarp even refers to Ephesians 4:26 as "scripture." But since this is the only time where he so designates a New Testament passage, and since he connects it with a passage found in Psalms, it has been suggested that Polycarp made an error of memory, mistakenly thinking that the Ephesians statement was from the Psalm.[46] There does not seem to be any way of knowing whether or not Polycarp *intended* to refer to Ephesians as "scripture." Two important conclusions about the developing canon can be drawn from Polycarp, however. It is clear that he used many New Testament writings as authoritative in some sense.[47] But he apparently did so

[43] Ibid., 58.

[44] Ibid., 60.

[45] Ibid., 61.

[46] Robert M. Grant, *The Formation of the New Testament* (New York: Harper & Row, 1965) 105.

[47] Ibid., 105–06.

without regarding them as uniquely "canonical," that is, as being clearly set apart from the rest of the tradition.[48]

Two more early-second-century writings remain to be considered; they are the Shepherd of Hermas and 2 *Clement*. In the Shepherd, there are clear references to New Testament themes and statements, but no explicit quotations from any canonical writings.[49] Grant has remarked that Hermas' "fondness for apocalyptic thought and literature takes him far beyond any concern for ideas of canonicity."[50] Also, Hermas' discussion of "the apostles and bishops and teachers and deacons," some of whom have "already fallen on sleep, and others still living" (3.5), would seem to indicate his loyalty to persons of authority rather than to a written canon only.

Finally we consider 2 *Clement*. The author of this work combines sayings of Jesus found in the soon-to-be canonized Gospels, but it is unclear what his sources are.[51] He does quote either Matthew 9:13 or Mark 2:17 with the introductory formula "again another scripture saith" (2.4). But his use of the sayings of Jesus is not limited to those that are found in the gospel canon of the later Church. For example, in paragraph 12 the author says,

> For the Lord Himself, being asked by a certain person when His kingdom would come, said, "When the two shall be one, and the outside as the inside, and the male with the female, neither male nor female."

Though not found in the Gospels of Matthew, Mark, Luke, or John, this saying is remarkably similar to a saying found in the Gospel of Thomas which reads,

> Jesus said to them, "When you make the two into one, and when you make the inner like the outer and the outer like the inner, and the upper like the lower, and when you make male and female into a single one, so that male will not be male nor the female be female. . . ."[52]

It is true that the author of 2 *Clement* appeals to "the Books and the Apostles" as authoritative in his discussion of the nature of the Church

---

[48] Ibid.

[49] Ibid., 72–75.

[50] Ibid., 75.

[51] Metzger, *The Canon*, 67–70.

[52] Gospel of Thomas 22.4-5 in Robert J. Miller, ed., *The Complete Gospels* (Sonoma: Polebridge Press, 1987).

(14.2). Metzger notes that while it is uncertain whether the reference to "apostles" should be understood as oral or written authority, it is most likely either oral or both oral and written, since the apostles do not fall under the rubric of the "books."[53]

So, what may be said of the status of the developing New Testament canon by the middle of the second century? It would seem that although many New Testament writings were known, used, and regarded as authoritative in some sense at this time, there did not yet exist a closed collection of Christian writings equal in status and authority to the Old Testament within the developing catholic Church. Oral tradition, written documents, and a primitive form of apostolic succession were all sources of authority in the Church of the early second century. If there was anything like a written canon it would have been a collection of Paul's letters, but it would not have been clearly defined nor would it have held any kind of exclusive authority.

3. Late Second Century

Much of the development of the New Testament canon appears to have taken place during the middle and latter parts of the second century. One witness to the development of the canon during this period is Justin Martyr. Gamble notes that, although individual Gospels had originally become locally well established and esteemed and that the traditional use of only one such document militated against the valuation of more than one gospel, Justin Martyr provides the first clear evidence of the knowledge, use, and esteem of several Gospels.[54] He regularly designates the Gospels as "memoirs of the apostles." For example, in his *First Apology* he declares that "the apostles, in the memoirs composed by them, which are called Gospels, have thus delivered unto us what was enjoined upon them . . ."(66). Gamble has concluded that Justin was acquainted with Matthew and Luke, and probably Mark also.[55] Also in his *First Apology* Justin declares that these "memoirs of the apostles" are read in public Christian worship services on Sundays, along with the "writings of the prophets" (67). Furthermore, Justin uses the word "gospel," which in the early period had been primarily a theological term, to refer to a written text *(Dial. 100)*. Gamble has noted, however, that Justin often cites traditions about Jesus which do not occur in the canonical Gospels and thereby "betrays a familiarity with a broader body of materials which he did not hesitate

---

[53] Metzger, *The Canon*, 71.
[54] Gamble, *NT Canon*, 28–29.
[55] Ibid., 28.

to use."[56] Beyond the Gospels, Justin provides us with the first clear and direct witness to the use of the book of Revelation.[57]

Another key witness to the development of the canon during the latter part of the second century is Irenaeus (ca. 185 C.E.). He provides us with the first evidence of a collection of the four canonical Gospels, as well as a defense of their (theoretically) exclusive authority.[58] In regard to this, Irenaeus asserts,

> It is not possible that the Gospels can be either more or fewer than they are. For, since there are four zones of the world in which we live, and four principal winds . . . it is fitting that [the Church] should have four pillars. . . . From which fact, it is evident that the Word . . . has given us the Gospel under four aspects, but bound together by one Spirit. . . . For the cherubim, too, were four-faced. . . . These things being so, all who destroy the form of the Gospel are vain, unlearned, and also audacious; those, [I mean,] who represent the aspects of the Gospel as being either more in number than as aforesaid, or, on the other hand, fewer (*Adv. Haer.* 3.11.8-9).

From this defense of a fourfold gospel it is clear that by the end of the second century these four Gospels were becoming an authoritative collection in catholic Christianity. But Gamble notes that Irenaeus' need to produce such a "tortured" defense of the collection implies that there was, in fact, opposition to the idea.[59] This observation is supported by the fact that Marcion had canonized only one gospel, and by the fact that Tatian had produced his *Diatessaron* (a synthesis of the four Gospels into one), the preference for which endured a long time in Syria.[60]

---

[56] Ibid., 29.

[57] Ibid., 46. For Justin's use of Revelation, see *Dial. 81.*

[58] Gamble, *NT Canon,* 31.

[59] Ibid., 31–32. Though Irenaeus' defense does seem a bit extravagant to the modern mind, it should be noted that numbers had much symbolic significance in the ancient world (and for some in the modern world as well), including the number four which symbolized universality. This is evidence that the developing New Testament canon is a catholic construction; that is, Irenaeus recognizes the need for more than one witness to the life of Jesus. Witnesses from churches around the Mediterranean are important to him. For a discussion of the sacred significance of the number four from a modern psychological perspective, the interested reader is referred to Carl Jung's rather lengthy discussion in *Psychology and Religion* (New Haven, Conn.: Yale University Press, 1938/1966 reprint). Cf. Maureen Tilley, "Typological Numbers: Taking a Count of the Bible," *Bible Review* (June 1992) 48–49.

[60] See Irenaeus, *Adv. Haer.* 3.11.9, and Gamble, *NT Canon,* 30.

In addition to the Gospels, Irenaeus refers to Acts, Paul's letters, and the Shepherd of Hermas as "scripture" (*Adv. Haer.* 3.12.9, 12; 4.20.2). Bruce concludes that Irenaeus' New Testament canon consisted of twenty-two books, including the four Gospels, Acts, Paul's letters (excluding Hebrews), 1 John, 2 John, 1 Peter, and Revelation,[61] and to this list Hoover adds the Shepherd of Hermas.[62]

But is Irenaeus' primary concern the establishment of a literary canon per se? The answer is clearly no. Irenaeus was primarily interested in solidifying and defending the "rule of faith" which was shared by other catholic writers like Tertullian. The rule of faith was an established set of theological beliefs, generally trinitarian in form, which Irenaeus believed was confessed in the Church throughout the entire world. The rule of faith was supreme, the New Testament documents serving the twofold purpose of expounding and proving it.[63] The primary means of defining and defending the rule, however, was not written testimony, but living (oral) testimony. After listing by name the bishops who had participated in the apostolic succession, Irenaeus declares that it is by this succession that truth is established (3.3.3; 3.4.1). So with Irenaeus, a genuine, written New Testament canon has begun to emerge; however, it still does not possess exclusive or ultimate authority.[64]

Another important witness to the state of the canon at the end of the second century is the Muratorian Canon.[65] It is a list of all the Chris-

---

[61] F. F. Bruce, *The Canon of Scripture* (Downers Grove, Ill.: InterVarsity Press, 1988) 177.

[62] Roy W. Hoover, "How the Books of the New Testament Were Chosen," *Bible Review* (April 1993) 45. Metzger also implies that Irenaeus had twenty-two books in his canon, but he excludes Philemon and implies that the canon included James. The implied inclusion of James is apparently an oversight on the part of Metzger, as Jacobean scholars are fairly unanimous in their conclusion that no Father before Origen in the third century used James as Scripture. For a good overview of the reception and use of James in the early Church, see Luke Timothy Johnson, *The Letter of James: A New Translation with Introduction and Commentary* (New York: Doubleday, 1995) 124–40.

[63] Lee Martin McDonald, *The Formation of the Christian Biblical Canon* (Nashville: Abingdon Press, 1988) 93.

[64] Tertullian, in his *Prescription Against Heretics*, 8–30, argues in a similar and detailed manner for the nature and supremacy of the rule of faith. The Scriptures are the "records of the faith" but the common theological confession of the churches is supreme and proven valid and trustworthy for Tertullian by, among other things, the uniformity of the deposit of tradition which was deposited in the churches by the apostles.

[65] The following observations are made based upon the assumption that the Muratorian Canon list was composed around 200 C.E., a date accepted by most New

tian writings which were accepted as authoritative in the Church. Included on the list are the four Gospels, Acts, thirteen Pauline epistles (Hebrews not included), two Johannine epistles (1 John and one of the two smaller ones), Jude, and Revelation. Also included are the Wisdom of Solomon and, with some reservation, the Apocalypse of Peter. The Shepherd of Hermas is recommended for private reading but is disallowed as a document for public reading in the Church because of its recent composition.[66]

This canon list is evidence that the New Testament was well on its way toward being solidified by the end of the second century. However, we cannot conclude that the canon had "already reached [its] final form and significance" by this time as von Campenhausen claims.[67] First of all, there was apparently still some controversy surrounding the Gospels. After explaining the origins of the four Gospels, the author of the Canon states: "And therefore, though various rudiments are taught in the several Gospel books, yet that matters nothing for the faith of believers, since by the one guiding Spirit everything is declared in all. . . ." Gamble notes that the defense of the four Gospels in the text of the canon is further evidence that a fourfold Gospel was still the object of some criticism.[68] Second, it should be noted that Hebrews, James, 1 Peter, 2 Peter, and one of the Johannine epistles are absent from the list. And third, the rather extensive nature of this list is something of an anomaly before the fourth century and as such it cannot be used to draw conclusions concerning the developing canon for the entire Church of the early third century.

The writings of other Christian leaders of the late second and early third centuries reveal that the process of canonization was still not complete. For example, Clement of Alexandria regarded the content of the Shepherd of Hermas as having been divinely revealed. He quotes the work with the following introduction: "Divinely, therefore, the power which spoke to Hermas by revelation said . . ." (*Strom.* 1.29; cf. 1.17). Clearly the Shepherd was authoritative for Clement, as was the Gospel of the Hebrews and the Gospel of the Egyptians.[69] Tertullian (ca.

Testament scholars. A few have argued for a fourth-century date, the most notable being Sundberg. See Sundberg, "Revised History," 452–61; and "Canon Muratori," 1–41. For a refutation of Sundberg and defense of the consensus view, see E. Ferguson, "Canon Muratori," 677–83.

[66] For a full translated text of the Muratorian Canon, see Gamble, *NT Canon*, Appendix, from which all quotations are taken.

[67] Campenhausen, *Formation*, 327.

[68] Gamble, *NT Canon*, 33.

[69] Ibid., 34.

210 C.E.) too confirms the canonicity of the Gospels, Acts, the Pauline epistles, 1 Peter, 1 John, Jude, and Revelation, but he fails to cite James, 2 Peter, 2 John, or 3 John, and was unsure of the status of the Shepherd.[70]

What can be said about the shape of the canon at the end of the second century and beginning of the third? It is clear that the four Gospels, Acts, and the Pauline epistles had become canonical within many quarters of the catholic Church by this time. Beyond this, it appears that only 1 Peter and 1 John (and possibly Revelation) had been recognized as such to any significant extent. The heart of the canon had been established by the beginning of the third century, but there still did not exist anything like a clearly identifiable canon with fixed boundaries.[71]

4. Third Century

The third century provides little evidence of significant canonical development.[72] Origen of Alexandria (ca. 240 C.E.) provides evidence that the canon had developed slightly but was still not solidified. Eusebius has preserved Origen's comments on the authority of many Christian writings.[73] The works which were authoritative for Origen include the four Gospels, Acts, Paul's epistles, Hebrews (though he denied its Pauline authorship), 1 Peter, 1 John, Jude, and Revelation.[74] He also noted that 2 Peter was "doubtful" and that 2 and 3 John were disputed in the Church (*E.H.* 6.25). Furthermore, he used James, Jude, Barnabas, the Shepherd of Hermas, the Acts of Paul, the *Didache,* and *1 Clement,* and quoted "numerous traditions from unknown sources."[75] Other disputes over the authority of various New Testament documents took place throughout various regions during the third century.[76]

5. Fourth Century

This leads us into the fourth century, when the shape of the New Testament canon finally became solidified. The contributions of two

---

[70] Metzger, *The Canon,* 159–60.

[71] Gamble, *NT Canon,* 49–50.

[72] Ibid., 50–53.

[73] See esp. *E.H.* 6.25.

[74] Metzger, *The Canon,* 141.

[75] Gamble, *NT Canon,* 50–51. There is some disagreement among scholars over the canonical status of James for Origen. Metzger (ibid.) argues that Origen "expressed reservation" concerning the epistle. However, Johnson argues that Origen "championed James vigorously, including him in his canon. . . ." See Johnson, *The Letter of James,* 130.

[76] Gamble, *NT Canon,* 51–52.

major figures of this period are especially significant. The first is Eusebius. Writing during the first half of the fourth century, Eusebius provides valuable information about the state of the canon in his own time. Eusebius divides the writings of the Church into four categories (*E.H.* 3.25). These basic categories are "accepted" *(homologoumenois)*, "disputed" *(antilegomenōn)*, "rejected" *(nothois,* i.e., orthodox but non-canonical), and the "fictions of heretics" *(hairetikōn andrōn anaplasmata).*[77] Those which are, according to Eusebius, everywhere accepted include the four Gospels, Acts, the epistles of Paul, 1 Peter, and 1 John (*E.H.* 3.25). He indicates that for some, Revelation belongs in this category, and for others it belongs among the rejected. Among the disputed, which he says "are nevertheless recognized by many," are James, Jude, 2 Peter, 2 John, and 3 John. The rejected include the Acts of Paul, the Shepherd of Hermas, the Apocalypse of Peter, Barnabas, the *Didache*, and the Gospel of the Hebrews (and for some, Revelation). Those writings which Eusebius classifies as heretical include the *Gospel of Peter*, the *Gospel of Thomas*, the *Gospel of Matthias* (and "others besides them"), and various "Acts" of various apostles. Clearly then, even in Eusebius' day, "the question of the scope of Christian scripture was still a lively one. . . ."[78]

The first list of writings which is identical to our New Testament is found in the writings of Athanasius.[79] In his *Thirty-ninth Easter Letter,* written in 367 C.E., he declares:

> Again it is not tedious to speak of the books of the New Testament. These are, the four Gospels, according to Matthew, Mark, Luke, and John. Afterwards, the Acts of the Apostles and Epistles (called Catholic), seven, viz. of James, one; of Peter, two; of John, three; after these, one of Jude. In addition, there are fourteen Epistles of Paul, written in this order. The first, to the Romans; then two to the Corinthians; after these, to the Galatians; next, to the Ephesians; then to the Philippians; then to the Colossians; after these, two to the Thessalonians, and that to the Hebrews; and again, two to Timothy; one to Titus; and lastly, that to Philemon. And besides, the Revelation of John. These are fountains of salvation, that they who thirst may be satisfied with the living words they contain.

[77] Literally, "the imaginations of factious men." Some scholars prefer to see the division as threefold because of a perceived lack of clarity on the part of Eusebius. He says that the rejected "may be reckoned among the disputed books" but seems to indicate that he prefers the fourfold division outlined above. See Metzger, *The Canon,* 203–06, for a discussion of the issues related to Eusebius' classification.

[78] Gamble, *NT Canon,* 53.

[79] Bruce, *The Canon,* 209.

What happened between the writing of Eusebius' *Ecclesiastical History* and the issuance of Athanasius' letter? Is there anything that might explain the transition from uncertainty to certainty regarding the precise shape of the canon? Not long after Constantine had moved the capital of the empire to Byzantium (renamed Constantinople) in 330 C.E., he asked Eusebius to produce fifty Bibles for use in the churches there. While the sources do not tell us explicitly the effect this may have had on the shape of the canon, it seems clear that Eusebius would have had to make a decision regarding which New Testament documents to include. Apparently he decided to include both the "accepted" and "disputed" works listed above. The support which Constantine would have given to his decision would explain the subsequent and relatively universal acceptance of these twenty-seven books throughout the Church.[80] Although explicit evidence is lacking, this theory appears to be the only satisfactory explanation of the change that occurred during this period.

Though Athanasius' list would eventually be approved by such Church councils as the Council of Hippo in 393 and the Council of Carthage in 397, and would eventually be considered a "closed" canon in theory for most of the Church, it should be noted that even after Athanasius, disputes over the exact contents of the New Testament continued, especially in the East.[81] Nevertheless, by common consent over time these twenty-seven books became the primary authoritative writings of the catholic Church in its various forms.[82]

The Transverse Axis of Canon

This overview of the development of the New Testament canon in the early Church makes it clear that any use of the word "canon" to describe Scripture in this period must be qualified in two ways. First, there is the issue of *time*. At what point is it appropriate to designate a text as "canonical" and what is meant by that designation? When Clement of Rome uses a Pauline epistle in an authoritative manner in the last decade of the first century, was the text "canonical" for him? If so, was it canonical in the same manner as it was for Athanasius in the late fourth century? Second, there is the issue of *theory versus practice.* That is, does the theoretical description of a text by any given Church Father match the actual use of that text (or other "noncanonical" texts)

---

[80] See the discussion in Bruce, *The Canon,* 203–05.

[81] McDonald, *Formation,* 144.

[82] Those forms being the Eastern Orthodox, Roman Catholic, and Protestant branches of the Church.

by the same author? For example, when Athanasius describes the canonical collection as in some sense complete, does he really use only
these as authoritative biblical texts? This issue is real, for as Bruce
points out, even though Athanasius makes formal distinctions between
canonical and apocryphal Old Testament texts, in practice he appears
to have paid little attention to the formal distinction, even introducing
noncanonical texts at times with the formulae "the scripture says" and
"as it is written."[83]

This twofold qualification with regard to the use of the word
"canon" in the early period can best be illustrated by the following
graph:

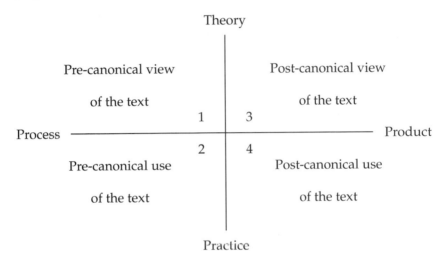

Illustration 1: The Transverse Axis of Canon

Quadrants 1 and 2 illustrate the tension that exists between theory
and practice before a particular text has secured for itself a relatively in-
disputable place in the canon, while quadrants 3 and 4 represent the
same tension after the text has found such a place. When does the
change take place? What is clear from the preceding historical overview is that each text has its own canonical history so that the time of
transition from pre-canonical to (post-)canonical varies from text to
text. It appears that in the early Church the lists of "canonical" texts
imply not absolute difference but *relative certainty and safety*. That is, in

---

[83] Bruce, *The Canon*, 80.

the patristic understanding of Scripture, to declare a text "canonical" is to say that it certainly teaches apostolic doctrine and is safe to use in worship, theology, and polemical disputation. This explains the simultaneous felt need on the part of the Fathers to create a literary canon *and* their inability to remove these texts from the broader stream of oral and written tradition. By the end of the fourth century it is fairly safe to say that for most of the catholic world, the twenty-seven books of the New Testament had achieved theoretical "canonical" status, although in practice some texts have always (even to this day) carried more weight in the Church's use of Scripture. But before this time no particular date can be assigned to the canonization of all the New Testament documents. For example, the various Gospels appear to have achieved more and more prominence individually in various parts of the Mediterranean world before Irenaeus' promotion of the fourfold gospel collection. After his time, these four Gospels were fairly secure in the developing canon throughout the Church. Therefore, it is reasonable, in my view, to claim that the Gospels achieved "canonical" status at the end of the second century. Other texts achieved this status much later, in light of the above identification of the biblical canon as a catholic canon, that is, as a canon accepted throughout the Church, both Eastern and Western. For example, I would argue that books like 2 Peter, Hebrews, and Revelation received this status during the middle and latter parts of the fourth century. Some churches accepted the authority of these writings earlier, of course, but their broad acceptance did not occur until this later period. The book of Acts appears to have had the shortest canonical history of all the New Testament documents, based upon the surviving evidence. It appears to have come on the scene, so to speak, rather suddenly with the work of Irenaeus and was never seriously disputed as a "canonical" document after his time within catholic circles.[84] The evidence would lead us to believe, therefore, that Acts achieved canonical status at the end of the second century.

All of this makes it necessary to refer to the "canon" in the first four centuries of the Church's history with care and nuance. Sundberg's distinction between "Scripture" and "canon" offers one method of handling the problem, but, as noted above, the distinction has not been accepted by the majority of biblical scholars. I maintain that the best way to reflect these historical ambiguities is to refer to the New Testament as

---

[84] Of course, the influence of Acts may have grown steadily throughout the second century, as the evidence from the early and mid-second century does not allow for firm conclusions. For an overview of the possible history of Acts during this period see Ernst Haenchen, *The Acts of the Apostles: A Commentary* (Philadelphia: The Westminster Press, 1971) 3–14.

"the developing canon" before the middle of the fourth century, and as "the canon" from the middle of the fourth century on. The development of the canon in the early Church can be likened to the growth of a human being, which is, of course, gradual in nature. In this analogy, the canon is in infancy during the first century, grows during the early and middle parts of the second century, hits a "growth spurt" during the late second century, and reaches adulthood during the fourth century. In light of this, I refer to the pre-fourth-century New Testament as "the developing canon."

The Canonical Critical Method

The primary method used throughout this study is canonical criticism, the latest historical method to be applied to the texts of Scripture. The primary historical methods that have traditionally been applied to the texts of Scripture include source, form, and redaction criticism. The New Testament source critics (such as B. H. Streeter and his successors) attempt to identify the sources used by the various biblical authors. Form critics (like Bultmann and Dibelius) have attempted to identify specific forms within the text and to discover the *Sitz im Leben* of those (primarily oral) forms within the early Christian communities. Redaction critics (like Bornkamm, Marxsen, and Conzelmann), building (to a certain extent) upon the results of the source and form critics, attempt to identify the characteristics of the final form of each text vis-à-vis their sources and counterparts. A classic example is the similarities and differences noted between the Gospels of Matthew and Luke, who, according to most scholars, used at least some of the same sources. While form criticism has waned a bit during the latter part of the twentieth century, source and redaction criticism continue to be applied vigorously to the New Testament by scholars, especially (but not exclusively) to the texts of the Gospels. Koester, for example continues to develop and apply both methods in his work on the Gospels, both canonical and noncanonical.[85]

The development of canonical criticism over the past thirty years represents the next logical step in the move from source and form criticism to redaction criticism. The canon critic recognizes the profound but previously underrecognized fact that the history of the text did not end with the work of the redactor. Rather, that history continued as the text was canonized and interpreted by the early Church, and it continues to this day in the communities that value and use the text. Canonical

---

[85] Helmut Koester, *Ancient Christian Gospels: Their History and Development* (Philadelphia: Trinity Press International, 1990).

criticism has been associated primarily with James Sanders and Brevard Childs.[86] While the former emphasizes historical and hermeneutical issues and the latter theological, both scholars are interested in the process of canonization and in the implications of that process for the modern interpreter. For example, Sanders, in his work on the canonical-critical method, proposes a system of interpretation which he identifies as "canonical hermeneutics." He proposes this after he describes the process of canonization. He attempts to identify and apply principles of interpretation that are directly based upon his understanding of the development of the canon, especially the observation that within the canon itself traditions are "adapted, represented, and resignified."[87] The result is a system of interpretation that, within broad theocentric bounds, is dynamic rather than static.

Building on the work of Sanders and Childs are scholars like Outler, Levering, Brenneman, Wall, and Lemcio.[88] Outler maintains that the new postmodern ecumenism calls for a new approach to the phenomenon of Scripture, arguing that the traditional Protestant-Catholic quarrels and the Enlightenment enthronement of autonomous reason have both placed the study of the canon into largely polemical contexts. Outler has called for an understanding of the development of the canon that takes into account the context of the early Church's search for identity and differentiation within its Hellenistic milieu.[89] Furthermore, he makes it clear that one need not reject the results of traditional historical criticism in the application of canon criticism; rather, he maintains that the results of canon criticism should be viewed as significant additions to the results obtained by those methods and to the study of early Church history in general.[90] It is his hope that canon criticism "might

---

[86] James Sanders, *Torah and Canon* (Philadelphia: Fortress Press, 1972); idem, *Canon and Community: A Guide to Canonical Criticism* (Philadelphia: Fortress Press, 1984); idem, *From Sacred Story to Sacred Text* (Philadelphia: Fortress Press, 1987); Brevard S. Childs, *The New Testament as Canon: An Introduction,* 2nd ed. (Valley Forge, Pa.: Trinity Press International, 1994).

[87] Sanders, *Canon and Community,* 47.

[88] Albert C. Outler, "The 'Logic' of Canon-making and the Tasks of Canon-criticism," *Texts and Testaments: Critical Essays on the Bible and Early Church Fathers,* ed. W. E. March (San Antonio: Trinity University Press, 1980) 263–76; Miriam Levering, "Introduction: Rethinking Scripture," *Rethinking Scripture: Essays from a Comparative Perspective,* ed. M. Levering (Albany: SUNY Press, 1989); R. W. Wall and E. E. Lemcio, *The New Testament as Canon: A Reader in Canonical Criticism* (Sheffield: JSOT Press, 1992).

[89] Outler, "The 'Logic' of Canon-making," 264.

[90] Ibid., 266.

help turn our inquiries in new directions, with a fresh set of queries and nuances."[91]

Levering argues that Scripture is best understood as "relational."[92] While traditional Scripture studies have focused on texts as objective, static entities, she maintains that sacred texts are better understood as *received* texts rather than as things in and of themselves. The impetus behind this shift for her is the nature of hermeneutics, that is, the need to reinterpret ancient texts in each new situation. Furthermore, she calls for the comparative study of various Scriptures in order to better understand the phenomenon of sacred text in all its multivalence. Thus, she has collected essays on the phenomenon of Scripture from scholars of various religious perspectives. Based upon their findings, she has identified six polarities which are found in the reception of sacred texts, including the tensions between *form and fluidity* (the identifiability of the text *and* its simultaneous change over time), *orality and writtenness, boundedness and openness, vectoring and being vectored* (that is, serving to carry the tradition and being carried by that tradition), *supernatural status and historical contingency,* and *normativity and selection/reinterpretation* ("canon with the canon"/new understandings of old texts).

Consciously building upon the work of Sanders, Brenneman maintains that the basic presupposition of the canon critic is the existence of difference within the canon, a difference that reflects the nature of reality. He maintains that the particular communities which canonize divergent texts do and should exercise the highest level of authority over the "functions" (rather than the "meanings") of texts. The community must choose between competing "canonical" voices within Scripture based upon the considerations of its own situatedness in time and space. The value of the canon, from this perspective, lies in the paradigmatic nature of the intracanonical debates that it contains, debates which are inherently communal. A primary example of this for Brenneman is the radically different understandings of the end of history which he finds in Isaiah 2:4 ("They shall beat their swords into plowshares") and Joel 3:10 ("Beat your plowshares into swords"). Drawing upon his own pacifist Mennonite tradition, Brenneman argues for the superiority of the former. In his work, canonical criticism functions as a communal variant of reader-response interpretation.[93]

Wall and Lemcio are attempting to transform the insights gained from traditional historical criticism into principles for contemporary

---

[91] Ibid., 271.

[92] Levering, "Rethinking Scripture," 1–17.

[93] James E. Brenneman, *Canons in Conflict: Negotiating Texts in True and False Prophecy* (New York: Oxford University Press, 1997).

biblical interpretation. They propose to do this through the investigation of the "earliest history of the church's relationship with its biblical canon. . . ."[94] Like Brenneman, they understand the diverse voices of the Bible as engaged in a sort of "conversation" that provides a model for contemporary interpretation. The current focus on intertextuality is magnified, in their view, by canon criticism, for it takes seriously the use of Scripture at each stage of the text's history.[95] From this point of view, to understand the early Church's use of Paul, for example, is to understand something of the early Church's use of Isaiah whose texts are found in the epistles of Paul. In this sense the interpretive process parallels the canonical process and provides hermeneutical insights for the modern interpreter.

In addition to the variations of canonical criticism outlined above, Barton argues that the greatest potential for the fruitfulness of the method lies in the direction of literary criticism. He argues that Childs' insistence upon reading the canon as a literary unit is on a par with the new literary approach to texts. From this perspective, texts ought to be read as units that contain meaning on their own apart from recourse to original historical context or authorial intention.[96]

In spite of the variations in the application of canonical criticism noted above, the common ground between all of these canonical-critical efforts lies: (1) in the recognition that the history of the biblical texts did not end with their "final" redaction, and (2) in the conviction that greater insight into the phenomenon of the canon is gained when the texts are understood in relation to their (early) interpreters than is gained when the texts are analyzed as entities in and of themselves (or in their constituent parts) in isolation from the canonizing community and its history. As Brenneman asserts,

> [Canonical criticism] seeks to account for both the historical critical life of a text/tradition *and* the interpretative journey of a text/tradition all along its route from sacred story to sacred text. [The method] . . . extends into the life of the believing communities throughout history.[97]

Brenneman also describes a primary difference between general canon studies in the traditional sense and the canonical-critical method of the

---

[94] Wall and Lemcio, *NT as Canon*, 16–17.

[95] Ibid., 18–19.

[96] John Barton, *Reading the Old Testament: Method in Biblical Study*, 2nd ed. (London: Darton, Longman and Todd Ltd., 1996) 89–103.

[97] Brenneman, *Canons in Conflict*, 15.

past thirty years as a shift "away from content to canonical function: *how* a community interpreted a tradition for its own particular setting."[98] This is the guiding principle of canonical criticism as it is applied throughout this project. In particular, I want to ask the question of the canonical function of one book within the canon: the book of Acts.

The problem with some recent attempts at the application of canonical criticism to the New Testament documents, however, as I see it, continues to be the tendency on the part of some scholars to analyze the texts of Scripture apart from the examination of other early non-canonical Christian texts; that is, without recourse to the broader history of the Church. This represents a continuation of the trend that has characterized post-Reformation New Testament studies in general. There is an irony, here, given the fact that a fundamental principle of the method is the examination of the post-redaction history of the text. The problem lies in the presentation of evidence taken from the final form of the canon alone, rather than from sources outside the canon, especially the writings of the Church Fathers and their theological opponents.

An example of this weakness can be seen in the works of Childs and Wall on the canonical significance of Acts. These canon scholars disagree with each other on the significance of the placement of Acts in the canon. The early lists of canonical documents display variety in the ordering of the New Testament writings. Sometimes Acts introduces the catholic epistles, and sometimes the Pauline epistles. Childs argues, on this basis, that the placement of Acts is insignificant, while Wall argues that the final placement of Acts after the Gospels and before the Pauline epistles is, in fact, of significance. Although these discussions are interesting and yield some valuable insights, it seems to me that an underlying problem with the discussion is the failure of both scholars to appeal to the writings of the Fathers themselves. Wall, for example, refers more than once to the "canonizing community" but does not identify particular persons or their writings; nor does he appeal to any Fathers for evidence. Both scholars argue for a rather limited unifying function for Acts somewhat reminiscent of Harnack, based upon the final form of the New Testament. Childs argues that the canonical significance of Acts lies in the context that it provides for the interpretation of the Pauline letters and for the strengthening of the unity of the Pauline corpus. Wall argues that the dividing of Luke's Gospel from Acts and the placing of Acts after the fourfold gospel corpus demonstrates the canonizing community's desire to read all four Gospels in

---

[98] Ibid., 137.

light of Acts. Furthermore, he argues that Acts provides a sort of commentary on the Pauline epistles as a result of its placement between the Gospels and epistles.[99]

The entire discussion needs to turn toward the writings of particular patristic figures. I will argue, based upon patristic evidence, that Acts did more than what these critics claim. It is my contention that in the eyes of the canonizing community, Acts unites the Old Testament, Gospels, Pauline epistles, and catholic epistles/Revelation and legitimizes a form of postapostolic hermeneutical authority all by means of its pneumatology. In this way it provided a basis for the Fathers to claim the entire canon as a unified witness to their developing trinitarian theology. It is my hope that at least a partial answer to the question of the canonization and function of the book of Acts within the early Church will be provided through the use of canonical criticism as an historical method.[100] Furthermore, I believe this study will provide at least a partial answer to the question of how a collection of diverse writings known today as the Bible was accepted and promoted in the Church as a unified corpus.

[99] See the discussions in Childs, *NT as Canon*, 228–40; and Wall and Lemcio, *NT as Canon*, 110–28.

[100] That is, while canonical criticism can address a number of historical, hermeneutical, literary, or theological concerns, it is my intention to produce results which answer historical questions related to the canonization of one particular text.

Chapter 1

The Patristic Use of Acts:
Late Second/Early Third Centuries

Scholars have long argued that the book of Acts was canonized at least in part because of the association of its traditional author, Luke, with the apostle Paul.[1] There is certainly merit to this observation, as patristic sources do contain arguments of this sort. The association of its author with an apostle undoubtedly gave the text *a priori* authority for those who accepted its Lukan authorship. But is this a sufficient explanation for the canonization of Acts? A similar argument was made by Irenaeus for the value of *1 Clement*. In *Against Heresies* 3.3.3, he claims that Clement, the third in the episcopal succession of the Roman church, had seen the apostles, had their preaching "echoing [in his ears]," and had their traditions "before his eyes." Furthermore, he asserts that Clement wrote "a most powerful letter to the Corinthians" in which he conveyed the apostolic teachings. And yet in the end, *1 Clement* did not become a part of the New Testament.

It is necessary to examine both the text of Acts itself and the patristic use of Acts to determine the value that the book had for the Fathers. The principle of value, identified by James Sanders in his use of canonical criticism, is the operative principle here.[2] What is it about Acts that secured for it a place in the patristic canon? Of what value was it to the developing catholic network of churches? What was its role vis-à-vis the other Scriptures? It is my thesis that Acts functioned for the fathers

---

[1] See, for example, Ernst Haenchen, *The Acts of the Apostles: A Commentary* (Philadelphia: The Westminster Press, 1971) 9.
[2] James Sanders, *Canon and Community: A Guide to Canonical Criticism* (Philadelphia: Fortress Press, 1984) 38.

both as the unifier of the developing biblical canon *and* as a justification for the episcopal claims of hermeneutical authority because of its pneumatology. That is, Acts provided a basis for the appropriation of *all* the biblical texts by the Fathers in their disputes with various Gnostic opponents, including the Marcionites. It functioned for them as the unifier of the developing biblical canon, and the value of Acts as a canonical unifier was established in the context of the claims of apostolic succession put forward by the Fathers—specifically Irenaeus and Tertullian. By claiming to be the inheritors of the teaching and traditions of the apostles, the catholics established for themselves the exclusive right of interpretation vis-à-vis their opponents. Simultaneous with their claim to own both the Scriptures and their proper interpretation, Irenaeus and Tertullian used Acts to demonstrate the unity of the divine message, and by so doing reinforced their use of the developing canon to support the "rule of faith." This foundational work of Irenaeus and Tertullian was adopted and developed by later Fathers and became a part of the catholic Church's perpetual identity and polemic.

Historical and Polemical Context

In order for the canonization and use of Acts by the Fathers of the late second and early third centuries to be understood, it is necessary to first establish the context in which this use took place. The second century C.E. was characterized by fierce disputes over the nature of Christian "orthodoxy" in terms of both content and ecclesiastical structure. That is, both the substance of Christian belief and the authority of the Church were being forged by different interpreters of the first-century Christian traditions. As Perkins notes, the interactions between catholics and Gnostics in the second century were likely facilitated by their common first-century heritage.[3] This observation raises the issue of the identification of "Gnosticism" as a historical or religious category. The legitimacy of such a designation is currently being challenged by some scholars.[4] Clearly the boundaries between the various catholic and

---

[3] Pheme Perkins, *Gnosticism and the New Testament* (Minneapolis: Fortress Press, 1993) 39.

[4] See, for example, Michael Allen Williams, *Rethinking "Gnosticism": An Argument for Dismantling a Dubious Category* (Princeton, N.J.: Princeton University Press, 1996). Williams argues that differences between groups traditionally designated as "Gnostic" are great enough to warrant the re-categorization of such groups. He suggests that many of the so-called "Gnostic" groups within the Christian tradition should be identified as "biblical demiurgical traditions" due to their dualistic theology. While Williams makes some excellent points, it seems to me that the traditional

Gnostic groups in the second century were not absolute. But in my view the categories are still historically legitimate and even necessary to distinguish between the various competing understandings of the world and the implications of these diverse understandings for the nature of Christian doctrine and the structure of the Church.

The best way to understand the distinctions between catholics and Gnostics in the second century is to view the competing interpretations of the inherited traditions as a spectrum. Christian Gnosticism appears to have developed largely in Alexandria, Rome, and Syria between 130 and 180 C.E. with the work of teachers like Basilides, Valentinus, Heracleon, and Menander.[5] Throughout the century, Gnosticism spread throughout the Mediterranean world.[6] Although no scholarly consensus has been reached on the precise origin or history of Gnosticism before the second century C.E., the phenomenon of Christian Gnosticism appears to be one result of the Christianizing of the Hellenistic-Jewish synthesis that had been taking place for some time (especially in Alexandria) and which is represented by the writings of Philo.[7] Gnostic teachers like Valentinus, one of the most significant of the second-century Gnostics, developed detailed metaphysical systems that set them apart from their second-century catholic counterparts. This highly developed Gnosticism differed from developing catholicism: (1) in its identification of the creator-god (Yahweh/Elohim) as different from and lesser than the Father of Christ; (2) in the various mythologies it created to explain this bifurcation; (3) in its rejection to one extent or another of both the created universe and the Scripture of Israel—a rejection which flowed from its dualistic theology; and (4) in its claim that only the Father of Christ (not the creator) could give the knowledge (gnosis) necessary for salvation. The specific manifestations of this ideology differed from teacher to teacher and from sect to sect, but these convictions appear to have been the basic point of departure for the various Gnostics in their attempt to resolve the ever-present philosophical "problem of evil."

The "Gnostic" category is complicated further still by the phenomenon of Marcionism. Marcion was born into a Christian family at Sinope,

---

"Gnostic" label is still useful so long as scholars make every reasonable effort to identify differences between the various Gnostic groups. His alternative phrase is quite cumbersome.

  [5] W.H.C. Frend, *The Early Church: From the Beginnings to 461*, 3rd ed. (London: SCM Press, Ltd., 1991) 82. This is not to suggest that Gnosticism originated in the second century—only that it became highly developed in its various forms.

  [6] Ibid., 51.

  [7] Ibid., 82.

in Pontus, Asia Minor, near the Black Sea.[8] After a dispute with the church there, he moved to western Asia Minor, but again left after his ideas found little acceptance. Marcion then went to Rome and joined a congregation there, donating a large sum of money to the church. After being excommunicated for his doctrines around 144 c.e. (and having his money returned), he founded his own church. Soon Marcionite churches sprang up throughout the Roman world. The heart of the dispute between Marcion and the catholics was the nature of the God of the Old Testament. In Marcion's view, the God of creation and of ancient Israel was not the same God as the Father of Christ, the God of the Christians. The former was vengeful and the cause of suffering, while the latter was pure mercy and love. Marcion rejected the writings of the Old Testament because he rejected the *God* of the Old Testament.[9] He claimed the apostle Paul as his authority, acknowledging abbreviated forms of the Gospel of Luke (which was associated with Paul) and ten Pauline epistles as his scriptural canon, and putting forth his now-lost *Antitheses* as the

---

[8] Biographical information and historical overview taken from Robert L. Wilken, "Marcion" and "Marcionism," *The Encyclopedia of Religion,* ed. Mircea Eliade, vol. 9 (New York: MacMillan Publishing Co., 1987) 194–96; and Johannes Quasten, *Patrology,* vol. 1 (Westminster: The Newman Press, 1951) 268–71.

[9] The Marcion known to us today is largely the reconstruction of Adolf von Harnack found in his magisterial work of 1924, *Marcion: The Gospel of the Alien God,* trans. J. Steely and L. Bierma (Durham: The Labyrinth Press, 1990 reprint). Elements of his sympathetic representation have been challenged recently by scholars, including the exaggerated credit given by Harnack to Marcion for the creation of the catholic biblical canon, the precise form of his reconstruction of Marcion's biblical text, his failure to see Marcionism as one form of Gnosticism, the "Protestant" nature of his Marcion, and his (Harnack's) overlooking of the apologetic need of the Christians to link their religious claims to antiquity. These kinds of critiques can be found in David L. Balas, "Marcion Revisited: A 'Post-Harnack' Perspective," *Texts and Testaments: Critical Essays on the Bible and Early Church Fathers,* ed. W. E. March (San Antonio: Trinity University Press, 1980) 95–108; John J. Clabeaux, *A Lost Edition of the Letters of Paul: A Reassessment of the Text of the Pauline Corpus Attested by Marcion* (Washington, D.C.: The Catholic Biblical Association of America, 1989); R. Joseph Hoffmann, *Marcion: On the Restitution of Christianity* (Chico: Scholars Press, 1984); Daniel H. Williams, "Harnack, Marcion and the Argument of Antiquity," *Hellenization Revisited: Shaping a Christian Response within the Greco-Roman World,* ed. W. E. Helleman (Lanham, Md.: University Press of America, 1994) 223–40; and David S. Williams, "Reconsidering Marcion's Gospel," *Journal of Biblical Literature* 108/3 (1989) 477–96. Although each of the criticisms listed above has merit, in my judgment the basic interpretation of Marcion given by Harnack remains credible and as such informs the conclusions drawn in this project with regard to the implications of Marcion's philosophy of canon.

proper interpretation of Scripture.[10] In Marcion's view, only Paul truly understood the message of Jesus, a message that included the rejection of the Law. The other apostles had mixed elements of Judaism with the new revelation, and could not be trusted. The message of Marcion of a purely loving God was attractive to many people. The movement spread and evidence of its success exists as late as the fifth century.

Was Marcion a "Gnostic"? As expressed above, it seems to me that the "spectrum" model provides us with the best way of understanding both the similarities and differences between the diverse interpreters of the Christian traditions during the second century. It appears that Marcion held strongly to the first and third Gnostic principles outlined above, namely, a version of theological dualism and the rejection of both the created world and the ancient Scriptures associated with the creator-god. He does not appear to have embraced the metaphysical speculations of the Valentinians and others like them, nor does he appear to have espoused the need for mystical gnosis in his soteriology. He did, however, claim that Jesus and Paul had brought the knowledge of the high God for the first time in history. For these reasons I classify Marcion as a Gnostic but with the understanding that he apparently did not espouse the detailed metaphysics and mystical tendencies of other Gnostics.

There may be an analogy from the modern world that can help to resolve this problem of categorization. Since the sixteenth-century Reformation in the Western Church, non-Roman Catholic Christians have been designated as "Protestants." Is this a legitimate category? Are there not significant differences between the various Protestant denominations? To be sure there are many, and these differences have produced (and continue to produce) disputes over matters of belief and practice. But the agreement between these groups on certain foundational

---

[10] Marcion's version of the New Testament excluded passages that linked Christian doctrine with the Old Testament or its God, or that seemed to legitimize the religion of Israel. Marcion claimed to have restored the text (which had been corrupted by Judaizing influences) to its original version, while the catholics charged him with textual mutilation, excising whatever failed to suit his theological fancies. For a textual-critical analysis of Marcion's version of the text, see Clabeaux, *Lost Edition*. Clabeaux is interested in reconstructing not only Marcion's text, but also Marcion's *vorlage*. He takes a minimalist approach with regard to ancient citations of Marcion's text, as opposed to Harnack's maximalist approach (5). That is, Harnack was interested in establishing as much of Marcion's text as possible, whereas Clabeaux is interested in establishing as much certainty as possible. With regard to Marcion's exclusion of the Pastoral epistles, it is unknown whether he knew them and rejected them as non-Pauline, or whether he simply was unaware of their existence, if, indeed, they had been composed by his time.

issues, it seems to me, renders the category legitimate so long as the differences are noted. The same would seem to be the case with regard to ancient Gnosticism.

The catholics were still in the process of developing their own ideology during the second century. Nevertheless, their common point of departure appears to have been the conviction that the creator-God is the God who redeems humanity through Christ, thus setting them apart from the various Gnostic groups. Therefore, they attempted to claim the Scriptures of the Creator (that is, the "Old Testament") as their own and to present their interpretation of Christ in light of those Scriptures. Thus catholicism represents the other end of the interpretive spectrum proposed above. Between these ends there appear to have been many varieties of Gnostic and catholic understandings— including a substantial overlap in both belief and practice. But these differences in presupposition should not be underestimated; indeed, they are crucial for understanding the polemics of the century and the place of Acts in those polemics.

Before the discovery of the Nag Hammadi codices in Egypt in 1945, scholars were dependent upon the writings of the catholic Fathers for their knowledge of second-century Gnosticism, writings that are self-evidently polemical. But as a result of the discovery of the Nag Hammadi documents, Gnostic ideas can now be studied from primary Gnostic sources.[11] The discovery produced forty-six documents of varying genres translated into Coptic from Greek originals, most of which represent varieties of second- and third-century Gnosticism.[12] The documents help to round out our understanding of the disputes that occurred during the second and third centuries between the catholics and Gnostics, as well as those that occurred between rival Gnostic groups. As Ehrman observes, "Not the least interesting thing about the Nag Hammadi tractates is that some of them engage in polemics against heretical tendencies of other groups, including the group that eventually acquired dominance. . . ."[13] Pearson notes that the Nag

---

[11] For an overview of Nag Hammadi scholarship as it relates to New Testament studies in general, see James M. Robinson, *Nag Hammadi: The First Fifty Years* (Claremont: The Institute for Antiquity and Christianity, 1995); and Perkins, *Gnosticism*.

[12] Birger A. Pearson, "Nag Hammadi," *The Anchor Bible Dictionary*, vol. 4, ed. David Noel Freedman (New York: Doubleday, 1992) 986–91. Unfortunately, our understanding of Marcion and his successors continues to be based on the writings of the catholics since his *Antitheses* have been lost and no known Marcionite writings were found at Nag Hammadi.

[13] Bart D. Ehrman, *The Orthodox Corruption of Scripture: The Effect of Early Christological Controversies on the Text of the New Testament* (New York: Oxford University Press, 1993) 9.

Hammadi corpus has expanded our knowledge of Gnostic theological polemics, confirming what we know from the catholic Fathers themselves "that certain gnostic sects spoke contemptuously of catholic Christians as . . . not [being] in possession of gnosis."[14]

Of tremendous relevance here is the tractate entitled *The Testimony of Truth (Testim. Truth)*. Based upon internal references to the Valentinians and the persecution of Christians, Pearson establishes the *terminus a quo* for the composition of the document as the mid-second century, and the early fourth century as the *terminus ad quem*. He then argues rather convincingly that *Testim. Truth* was probably written during the late second or early third century by the Gnostic Cassianus of Alexandria. His case is based upon detailed parallels that are found between the teachings of Cassianus and those promoted in *Testim. Truth*.[15] Whether Pearson is right in his authorial identification or not, *Testim. Truth* provides a "voice from the other side," so to speak, in the catholic-Gnostic debates of the day. Not only does *Testim. Truth* apparently come from the time of Irenaeus and Tertullian, it engages in similar kinds of polemics—but from what may be termed a "radical Gnostic perspective." The author bitterly denounces both the Valentinians and the catholics! Pearson is convinced that the author (Cassianus) was a former Valentinian who retained many Valentinian ideas after leaving the group. The reason for his departure was presumably his extreme asceticism, especially with regard to sexuality.[16]

One of the fundamental elements in the Gnostic-catholic disputes was the issue of religious authority. First, the nature, extent, and interpretation of the biblical canon were debated. Were the Scriptures of ancient Israel and Judaism authoritative for the Church? Should "apostolic" writings be placed alongside the Old Testament texts as Scripture? Should they replace the Old Testament? Should there be any written canon at all in the Church? These were the kinds of questions being asked both explicitly and implicitly—questions which received different answers from different interpreters of the first-century traditions.

Second, the nature and appropriation of apostolic teaching and authority also lay at the center of the debate between catholics like Irenaeus and Tertullian on the one hand, and their Valentinian and Marcionite opponents on the other. Did the apostles preach the "whole

---

[14] Birger A. Pearson, "Anti-Heretical Warnings in Codex IX from Nag Hammadi," *Essays on the Nag Hammadi Texts in Honour of Pahor Labib*, Nag Hammadi Studies, vol. 6 (Leiden: E. J. Brill, 1975) 145.

[15] Birger A. Pearson, "Introduction to IX.3: The Testimony of Truth," *Nag Hammadi Codices IX and X*, Nag Hammadi Studies, vol. 15 (Leiden: E. J. Brill, 1981) 117–20.

[16] Pearson, "Testimony," 118–19.

counsel of God" openly and to all? Did they preach *before* they had received spiritual enlightenment? Did they preach one thing publicly
and another thing privately to those who had achieved a higher level of
spiritual understanding? Was it their *method* of receiving revelation that
was authoritative or the *content* of their teaching? Was their teaching to
be learned by means of oral tradition or through written texts? All of
these questions were live ones throughout the second century when
Acts was first used by the catholics in their polemical disputes.

Perkins makes two primary observations concerning the appropriation of apostolic authority in the second century. First, she notes that
both the catholics and the Gnostics claimed apostolic authority in one
way or another. The particular apostles to which the Gnostics appealed
depended upon the group. In the *Gospel of Thomas,* Matthew and Peter
are presented as inferior to Thomas, but in the *Apocryphon of John, First
and Second Apocalypses of James,* the *Apocryphon of James,* and the *Apocalypse of Peter,* James and Peter are the primary sources of Gnostic teaching that had been rejected by the catholics.[17] Second, a profound shift
occurred during the late second century with the work of Irenaeus.
During most of the second century, arguments tended to be based on
traditions associated with *particular* apostles. Perkins notes that "the
argument for apostolic tradition was conducted on both sides by claiming descent from a single apostolic figure."[18] Even Irenaeus appeals to
Johannine authority in a special way for his own authority.[19] But this
general tendency changes with Irenaeus' use of Acts to argue for the
unity and anti-Gnostic nature of the teaching of the apostles.[20] After
Irenaeus, she argues, "[the] framework of some of the gnostic writings
has been formulated to address this type of argument."[21] The influence
of Irenaeus' use of Acts to appropriate all the apostles for his primitive
trinitarian theology is evident, she maintains, in works like the *Letter of
Peter to Philip* in which the apostles gather as a group and receive Gnostic revelation before they depart to preach throughout the world.[22] The
particulars of this development will be explicated below.

Internal Evidence

It is in this historical and polemical context that Acts is first used by
the catholics to argue for the unity of the Old Testament and the teach-

---

[17] Perkins, *Gnosticism,* 180.
[18] Ibid.
[19] Ibid., 180–81.
[20] Ibid., 181.
[21] Ibid.
[22] Ibid.

ings of Jesus and the apostles. When the structure of the Christian Bible is identified, clues to the role of Acts as a unifier of the developing catholic canon begin to emerge. If the key authoritative figures in biblical history are identified as the Israelite prophets, Jesus, Paul, and the Jerusalem apostles (Peter, John, and James the brother of Jesus), then we have a corresponding representation in the canon. The Old Testament represents the prophets,[23] the Gospels are identified with Jesus (not as author, but as subject matter), Paul's epistles represent Paul, and the catholic epistles and Revelation represent the Jerusalem apostles.[24] How does Acts fit into this canonical structure? It functions as the "glue" which holds all the pieces together; that is, as the unifier of the various

[23] While technically the Hebrew Bible was structured in a threefold manner (Law, Prophets, Writings), it is also common to find the entire corpus attributed to "prophets" by Jews and Christians in antiquity. This is especially true for the Christians who regularly referred to the Old Testament as "the prophets." This was due largely to the christological reading that Christians gave the Old Testament; the primary value of the entire corpus for them was its testimony to the coming of Christ. This is certainly evident in the writings of Luke. Sanders maintains that "Luke thinks of all the Scripture as something to be fulfilled—that is, as prophetic . . ." and that "when Luke thinks of the Scripture in general, as a unity, as the expression of the divine will, he says that it is prophetic." See Jack T. Sanders, "The Prophetic Use of the Scriptures in Luke-Acts," *Early Jewish and Christian Exegesis,* ed. C. Evans and W. Stinespring (Atlanta: Scholars Press, 1987) 191, 193. For a relatively comprehensive survey of Luke's use of Scripture in Acts, see John T. Carroll, "The Uses of Scripture in Acts," *Society of Biblical Literature 1990 Seminar Papers* 29 (1990) 512–28. Cf. James Barr, *Holy Scripture: Canon, Authority, Criticism* (Oxford: Oxford University Press, 1983) 54–56, for a good discussion of the fluidity of boundaries between "the Prophets" and "the Writings" in antiquity.

[24] In Galatians 2:9 Paul declares, "James, Peter, and John, those reputed to be pillars, gave me and Barnabas the right hand of fellowship" (NIV). The three major apostles from Jerusalem are called "pillars" *(stuloi)* and are identified in the following order: James, Peter, and John. Lührmann believes it is no coincidence that in the catholic epistles we have, in the same order, James, 1 and 2 Peter, and 1, 2, and 3 John. See Dieter Lührmann, "Gal. 2:9 und die katholischen Briefe," *Zeitschrift für Die Neutestamentliche Wissenschaft* 72 (1981) 65–87. He further argues that Jude's authority is derived from James based upon Jude 1 where the author claims to be the brother of James. (Thus in a sense Jude is to James what Mark is to Peter and Luke is to Paul—an associate who receives authority from the association.) Lührmann also argues that the final makeup of the catholic epistles was determined by the need for seven letters. (It is interesting to note that the Muratorian Canon claims that Paul wrote to seven churches just as John did in Revelation. In early Christianity the number seven was associated with completeness and universality as was the number four.) The reader should also note that Revelation is associated both with John and (loosely) with the catholic epistles in some patristic writings. The latter association is based upon the seven letters to the churches in chapters 2 and 3.

books. It takes in hand, so to speak, the "predictions" of the prophets of Israel (as represented by the Old Testament), the coming of the Messiah (as represented by the Gospels), the teachings of Paul (as represented by the Pauline epistles), and the teachings of the Jerusalem apostles (as represented by the catholic epistles and Revelation), and ties them all together by uniting the *texts* of the Old Testament with the authoritative *persons* of the New Testament—namely, Jesus, the Jerusalem apostles, and Paul.[25] And how does Luke do this? Certainly he does this through the skillful narration of key episodes in the story line. For example, Luke's narration of the Jerusalem council portrays Peter, Paul, and James as united in their decision regarding the duties incumbent upon the Gentiles who believe (Acts 15).[26] But I would argue that the unparalleled references to the Holy Spirit in Acts establish this unifying function above all else. Through the characterization of the Holy Spirit and the association of that Spirit with each "canonical" authority, Luke has constructed a paradigm that would provide the developing catholic hierarchy with a basis for appropriating the entire developing canon as a united witness to their theology.

Luke uses the motif of the Holy Spirit to "drive" the key characters in the story. The Spirit is mentioned between fifty-three and fifty-eight times in Acts, depending on some textual variants and disputed meanings. No other New Testament writing is comparable in this regard. The Greek word for spirit is *pneuma*, and its basic meanings include breath, breathing, and wind. These meanings associate the concept of Holy Spirit with the "breath" of God. For Luke, this image may have evoked the following scenes (among others): (1) the creation of the world in Genesis (with the Spirit hovering over matter while God speaks the creation into order); (2) the revitalization of Israel predicted by Ezekiel (as seen in the vision of dry bones coming to life); and (3) the divine inspiration of Israel's scriptures (as represented by Josephus and

---

[25] Luke wrote after the Old Testament had basically been canonized and the apostles had been recognized as authoritative figures, but before the writings attributed to the latter had been canonized. Most New Testament scholars do not believe that Luke used the Pauline epistles in his writing of Acts. Goulder, however, has proposed the theory that Luke knew and used 1 Corinthians and 1 Thessalonians. See Michael D. Goulder, "Did Luke Know Any of the Pauline Letters?" *Perspectives in Religious Studies* 13/2 (Summer 1986) 97–112.

[26] For discussions of Luke's literary skill in creating a unified narrative, see Marion L. Soards, *The Speeches in Acts: Their Content, Context, and Concerns* (Louisville: Westminster/John Knox Press, 1994); and Susan M. Praeder, "Jesus-Paul, Peter-Paul, and Jesus-Peter Parallelisms in Luke-Acts: A History of Reader Response," *Society of Biblical Literature 1984 Seminar Papers* No. 23 (Chico: Scholars Press, 1984) 23–39.

others). The image of divine breath or wind implies a moving of God in human affairs.

Luke's descriptions of the work of the Holy Spirit in Acts affirm his belief that the hand of God was behind the unfolding of each element in the story, and they serve to unify the prophets of ancient Israel, Jesus, the Jerusalem apostles, and Paul as each contributes to fulfillment of the divine will. The prophets of ancient Israel are credited with speaking by the Holy Spirit and with predicting the outpouring of the Spirit in the last days (1:16; 2:17; 28:25). Luke claims that Jesus had been anointed with the Holy Spirit, that he had given commands through the Holy Spirit, and that he had promised the outpouring of the Spirit after his ascension (1:2, 5; 10:38). The Jerusalem apostles receive the Holy Spirit, speak in tongues by the Spirit, preach with boldness by the Spirit, make predictions by the Spirit, and confer the Spirit on others (2:4; 4:31; 5:32; 8:17; 11:28). Paul is filled with the Spirit after his conversion and conducts the various aspects of his ministry by means of the Spirit. He is commissioned to evangelize by the Spirit, is empowered to perform miracles and preach by the Spirit, is forbidden to enter certain geographical areas by the Spirit, confers the Spirit on others *like the Jerusalem apostles do,* and is repeatedly warned by the Spirit about impending tribulations (9:17; 13:2, 9; 16:6-7; 19:6; 20:23; 21:4, 11).[27] All of these canonical authorities are joined together in various ways by the Spirit. They are all connected to the story of God's ancient and recent moving in human history by Luke. The Holy Spirit is the primary unifying principle in the book of Acts, driving the major figures in biblical salvation history and coordinating the outworking of the divine plan (1:8).

Dunn concludes that Acts is both "early catholic" and "enthusiastic" (i.e., charismatic) and that these two elements are held in tension.[28] But it seems to me that Luke actually uses pneumatology to strengthen the catholic nature of his work. The Spirit is granted by particular individuals—apostles who are themselves the primary ecclesiastical authorities in the text. In Acts, the Church controls the outpouring of the

[27] F. R. Harm argues that the structure of Acts itself can be determined by its pneumatology. The Spirit is first given by a sovereign act of Christ in a Semitic context (2:1-4), then granted by the laying on of hands by Peter and John (8:14-17). The Spirit is then given by another sovereign act of Christ in a Gentile context (10:44-45) and then granted by the laying on of Paul's hands (19:1-6). See F. R. Harm, "Structural Elements Related to the Gift of the Holy Spirit in Acts," *Concordia Journal* 14/1 (January 1988) 28–38. For a complete listing of the references to the Holy Spirit in Acts, see the Appendix, below.

[28] James D. G. Dunn, *Unity and Diversity in the New Testament: An Inquiry into the Character of Earliest Christianity,* 2nd ed. (Philadelphia: Trinity Press International, 1990) 357.

Spirit, except in a few pivotal episodes. The Spirit is bestowed by the apostles through the laying on of hands; those who are unworthy—in their judgment—are refused (8:14-25). The assumption by some scholars of an inherent tension between charismatic and ecclesiological religious expressions may be based on other pneumatological paradigms, like that apparently in operation in the church at Corinth, where charismatic expression appears to be highly individualized (1 Cor 12; 14). But in Acts the Spirit is the driving force behind the construction of the Church and the emphasis is on the orderly spreading of the apostolic message. This is seen even in Acts 2 where the phenomenon of tongues is intricately associated with the spreading of the message.

John Darr has recently concluded on the basis of a narrative-critical analysis of Acts that not only is the Holy Spirit a key character in Acts, but that Luke "develops and utilizes the Spirit largely as a means of building and maintaining coherence in a story that is potentially disjunctive."[29] Darr argues that there are both vertical and horizontal dimensions to this phenomenon. The former relates to the divine element in the narrative. How can Luke make God a key character in the story-line without violating the traditional doctrine of transcendence? The Spirit—the traditional belief in that aspect of the divine Being which is immanent throughout creation—is Luke's answer. Through the personification of the Spirit Luke assures his readers of the divine involvement in each aspect of the unfolding of the story.[30] Horizontally, Darr notes that Luke's story world is quite broad, "encompassing several distinct epochs and numerous human protagonists."[31] By his pneumatology, Luke attempts to demonstrate, among other things, a "continuity across the breadth and complexity of this horizon. . . ."[32] Darr concludes that Luke "harnesses the Spirit" in order to establish structure, order, and coherence, and by this means to instill certainty in his readers.[33] These findings reinforce my own conclusions concerning the structure of Acts and the role of the Spirit motif within that structure.

[29] John A. Darr, "Spirit and Power in Luke-Acts." An unpublished paper presented at the annual meeting of the Society of Biblical Literature in San Francisco, Calif. (November 22, 1997) 3.

[30] Ibid.

[31] Ibid.

[32] Ibid. As an interesting aside, it is quite possible that Luke's personification of the Spirit contributed to the later trinitarianism of the Church. Examples of this personification are found in Acts 5:3, where Ananias is accused of lying to the Holy Spirit, and in Acts 15:2, where the Spirit speaks to the Antiochene leaders.

[33] Darr, "Spirit and Power," 3. This reference to "certainty" by Darr is an allusion to Luke 1:4 where Luke declares his intention to provide Theophilus with "certainty" *(asphaleian)* concerning the things which he had been taught.

But there is another interesting use of pneumatology in Acts that will become significant as this study unfolds. Acts 18:18–20:38 records the ministry of Paul at Ephesus. After preaching in the synagogue, Paul discovers some disciples of John the Baptist who, after hearing Paul's message, are baptized in the name of Jesus. They then receive the Holy Spirit by the laying on of Paul's hands. After a lengthy teaching ministry in Ephesus, Paul leaves, only to return later to exhort the elders of the church. Calling for the elders to meet him in Miletus, he urges them to take heed to themselves and to the flock, over which the Holy Spirit had made them "bishops" *(episcopous)*. They are warned by Paul that certain "savage wolves" (i.e., false teachers) will arise and seek to create a following. The "bishops" must guard the flock from such as these. As will become clear in what follows, this passage—wherein Paul communicates the Spirit through the laying on of hands and this same Spirit appoints "bishops"—would eventually be used to reinforce the episcopal claim of apostolic succession. So by means of its pneumatology, Acts laid the foundation for the catholic Fathers to argue for both a unified canon *and* their own hermeneutical prerogative as successors to the apostles vis-à-vis the claims of the Gnostics.

With regard to the canonical question, however, it is not enough to examine the text of Acts itself. This brief examination of the pneumatological structure of Acts leads us to the primary application of the canonical-critical method. What remains to be done is a careful analysis of the use of Acts by the Church Fathers. It is my contention that Irenaeus and Tertullian establish the canonical function of Acts as the unifier of the developing canon through their polemical use of the text against their opponents. The value that Acts had for them can only be understood, however, when seen in the context of their claims to apostolic succession and the hermeneutical authority that accompanied these claims.

The Use of Acts in the Polemics of Irenaeus

The first significant use of Acts in the early Church is found in the writings of Irenaeus (ca. 185 C.E.) as a result of his disputes with Marcion and the Gnostics.[34] Irenaeus was born sometime between 140 and 160 C.E.

---

[34] Harry Y. Gamble, *The New Testament Canon: Its Making and Meaning* (Philadelphia: Fortress Press, 1985) 47. The date of the composition of Acts is difficult to determine. Although most scholars would suggest a date between 70 and 90 C.E. for both Luke and Acts, Koester suggests that Luke may have been written as late as (but no later than) 125 C.E. and that Acts "could have been written a decade later." H. Koester, *Introduction to the New Testament. Volume Two: History and Literature of*

in Asia Minor—probably Smyrna—and, according to evidence in Eusebius, as a youth had listened to sermons by Polycarp who was bishop
of Smyrna.[35] For unknown reasons, Irenaeus left Asia Minor and went
to Gaul in the West. As a presbyter there he was sent to Rome to mediate
in a Montanist dispute (ca. 177 C.E.). Shortly after returning, Irenaeus
became bishop of Lyons. The two literary works of Irenaeus that have
survived are *Against Heresies,* in which he refutes perspectives that he
considers heretical (especially Gnosticism), and *The Demonstration of the
Apostolic Teaching,* a summary and defense of the theology accepted by
Irenaeus.

In *Against Heresies,* Book 3, Irenaeus quotes extensively from the
book of Acts in an effort to demonstrate the unity of the God of Israel
and the God of the Christians, the unity of Jewish and Gentile believers, the unity of Jesus and Christ, and—most significantly here—the
unity of the apostolic teaching (including that of Peter, John, Paul, and
James).[36] Throughout Book 3, Irenaeus attempts to refute the Gnostics
in general and Marcion in particular (as well as the Ebionites and other
anonymous persons whom he considers heretical). He does this by establishing both the content of and the historical basis for the catholic
rule of faith, and he argues from both oral tradition and Christian texts
that were increasingly being recognized as authoritative within the
Church. Irenaeus is primarily arguing that the Creator—the God of
the Old Testament—is also the Redeemer, in opposition to the Gnostic
bifurcation of the two.

As noted above, one of the most outstanding documents among
the Nag Hammadi codices is *The Testimony of Truth (Testim. Truth).*

Early Christianity (Philadelphia: Fortress Press, 1982) 310. An early-second-century
date for the composition of Acts is possible. The catholic and conciliatory nature of
Acts fits nicely with this time period, as does Luke's use of pneumatology to unite
the biblical authorities and the "bishops" of Ephesus. The consensus of modern
scholars that Luke did not use the Pauline epistles in the construction of Acts, however, remains a formidable argument in favor of an earlier date. That is, it is difficult
to imagine that Luke could have constructed a text as late as 135 C.E. that gives so
much space to Paul without recourse to Paul's epistles, texts that by that time had
apparently been circulated to such an extent that Luke would have been hard
pressed to ignore them. Furthermore, the interest of Luke in theodicy in light of the
destruction of the Temple in 70 C.E. may also suggest an earlier date. Would the
Gentile Christians have waited so long to question the faithfulness of God in light of
this event? In light of all this, a first-century date for the composition of Acts seems
preferable.

[35] Biographical information taken from Quasten, *Patrology,* Vol. 1, 287–90.

[36] Unless otherwise noted, all quotations from the Church Fathers are taken
from the Eerdmans reprint edition.

Dated to the late second or early third century, it presents a radical Gnostic Christianity, engaging in both anti-Valentinian and anti-catholic polemics. As such, it helps the canon critic to situate the arguments of Irenaeus historically. In *Testim. Truth* 29.6ff., the author declares that he is speaking "to those who know to hear not with the ears of the body but with the ears of the mind."[37] "Truth" is contrasted with "the Law" throughout the treatise. Truth belongs to the author's Gnostic community, while the catholics are among those who adhere to the Law.[38] From the point of view of the author, the catholic acceptance of the authority of Genesis (with its sanctioning of physical procreation) binds them to the Law (29.11-15; 50.8) and to the inferior creator-god, and renders them "foolish" and of the "generation of Adam" (i.e., unspiritual). This loyalty to the God of the Old Testament renders the catholics incapable of understanding truth (29.9-15; 22-25) and "defiles" them through marriage and procreation (30.2-11). Jesus, the undefiled one, came to bring an end to this "dominion of carnal procreation" (30.18-30). The "word of truth" which he brings delivers the Gnostic believer from "ignorance" and "works of darkness" (31.5-15). The catholics are "foolish" for confessing Christ with their mouths but failing to demonstrate the power that comes to those who are freed from ignorance (31.22-28). Their foolishness is demonstrated by their willingness to suffer martyrdom—as if the Father desired human sacrifice. Martyrdom merely delivers them into the hands of the archons (30.28–32.22), and martyrs "bear witness only to themselves" (33.24-27). They deceive themselves by thinking, "If we deliver ourselves over to death for the sake of the Name we will be saved" (34.1-7). Furthermore, they demonstrate that they do not have the "word which gives [life]" (34.24-26) through their confession of a bodily resurrection (34.26–35.2). Christ saves those who renounce the "foolishness" of a carnal resurrection (36.3–37.1). Those who confess such a resurrection misunderstand the true nature of God's power and Scripture because they are double-minded (37.5-9), that is, guilty of confusing the material with the spiritual.

The author of *Testim. Truth* continues to condemn late-second-century catholic doctrine and practice by proclaiming that the word of Christ demands complete renunciation of the world and all human desire (41.2-13). The Gnostic is held out as the one who has been cleansed of all evil and filled with wisdom, counsel, understanding, insight, and

---

[37] Unless otherwise indicated, all quotations from the Nag Hammadi documents are taken from the Coptic Gnostic Library edited by James M. Robinson and published by E. J. Brill.

[38] Pearson, "Testimony," 102–07.

power (43.1-17). Salvation comes through knowledge of the self and of God; *this* is the "true testimony" (44.30–45.6). But it is the knowledge attainable through the author's sect that saves, not the knowledge of the Valentinians (55.1) nor that of other Gnostic groups associated in various ways with Valentinus, groups which practice "idol-worship" and procreation and which are confused (56.1–58.4).

After column 58 there are a number of lines missing in the surviving text. The author of *Testim. Truth* then condemns "heretics" *(haireticos)* and "schisms" *(schisma)*. Because of the lacunae it is not possible to determine with certainty the identity of these persons whom he condemns. What is significant, however, is that this Gnostic author is engaging in the same kinds of bitter polemics that the modern reader recognizes in the writings of the catholic polemicists. The late second century is a time during which there is fierce struggle for the establishment of a normative Christianity, with catholics and various groups of Gnostics all claiming the right for themselves and condemning their rivals as fraudulent.

It is in this historical context and against this kind of an alternative version of Christianity that Irenaeus constructs his case.[39] In arguing for the sole legitimacy of catholic beliefs and practices from the texts of the developing New Testament canon, he first uses the Gospels, then Acts, and finally the epistles (primarily but not exclusively those of Paul).[40] While my analysis will concentrate primarily on Irenaeus' extensive use of Acts, there are several relevant points in his use of the Gospels and epistles as well. Throughout the following review it will become clear that Irenaeus views the various biblical documents as being unified in their witness to the catholic rule of faith and that the book of Acts is central in his perspective, primarily because of its pneumatology.[41]

But Irenaeus' strategy is not simply one in which he delves immediately into Scripture for the purpose of proving his case. Rather, he first establishes his own hermeneutical authority so that in effect he has

---

[39] By "alternative version" I mean the Gnostic perspectives, including that of Marcion. This difficulty in classification is compounded even further by the fact that Irenaeus is addressing multiple opponents at once. But the common ground between most of them appears to be the theological dualism described above and its various ramifications, including its effect on the shape and interpretation of the biblical canon.

[40] This is the general order throughout Book 3; however, Irenaeus is somewhat lacking in organizational skill and periodically breaks the pattern.

[41] The argument of Irenaeus here is not that the biblical documents are unified on every point or in every detail, but that they all bear witness to the rule of faith.

declared himself the theological winner before the debate over Scripture has even begun. Although he begins Book 3 of his *Against Heresies* with the announcement that he is going to "adduce proofs from Scripture" (pref.), he soon makes an argument for the reality and priority of the apostolic succession. Central to his case is the claim that the apostles founded a number of churches around the Mediterranean world and appointed episcopal successors. These, in turn, were succeeded by others, who themselves were succeeded by other bishops, and this pattern continued down to his own time. After providing the list of the bishops in the church of Rome from Peter and Paul to his own day, Irenaeus declares that by means of this succession the apostolic tradition and preaching of "the truth" had come to him and to his fellow catholics. Then he boldly declares that this is the greatest proof that his faith is the one true apostolic faith (3.3.3). He continues by asking,

> Suppose there arise a dispute relative to some important question among us, should we not have recourse to the most ancient Churches with which the apostles held constant intercourse, and learn from them what is certain and clear in regard to the present question? For how should it be if the apostles themselves had not left us writings? Would it not be necessary, [in that case,] to follow the course of the tradition which they handed down to those to whom they did commit the Churches (3.4.1)?

The "faith" to which he refers is developing trinitarianism. Although not the full-blown trinitarianism of the fourth century, his own contribution to trinitarian theology was a large step in that direction. One of the clear expressions of Irenaeus' "rule of faith" is found in Book 1. In order to know exactly what it is that Irenaeus is so determined to defend, I reproduce the following statement of the rule. Irenaeus declares,

> The Church, though dispersed throughout the whole world, even to the ends of the earth, has received from the apostles and their disciples this faith: [She believes] in one God, the Father Almighty, Maker of heaven, and earth, and the sea, and all things that are in them; and in one Christ Jesus, the Son of God, who became incarnate for our salvation; and in the Holy Spirit, who proclaimed through the prophets the dispensations of God, and the advents, and the birth from a virgin, and the passion, and the resurrection from the dead, and the ascension into heaven in the flesh of the beloved Christ Jesus our Lord, and His [future] manifestation from heaven . . . that He should execute just judgment towards all . . . (1.10.1).

So before engaging in debates with his opponents over the proper confines of the canon and its interpretation, Irenaeus declares that the *churches* of the apostles have preserved the teaching of the apostles— and thus of Christ—and that this faith is trinitarian in nature.[42] In fact, he states that it is appropriate to examine the Scriptures in search of proof because the teaching of the apostles is found "in the Church" (3.5.1). The implication is that the "proper" interpretation is known before the textual examination has even begun; thus, he has created a scenario in which he cannot lose the debate.

Irenaeus' argument for the apostolic succession and its hermeneutical legitimacy reflects a basic difference in presupposition between the Gnostics and the catholics. For the former, the post-resurrection appearances (visions) of Christ to his followers were an ongoing phenomenon; something that those who were attaining the highest level of spiritual knowledge (gnosis) could claim for themselves. As Pagels notes, "Gnostic Christians [refused] to accept the canonical limitation of the appearances."[43] On the other hand, the catholics were less existential and more historical in their understanding of the appearances of the risen Christ and in the divine revelation(s) associated with those appearances. For them, the authority of the Twelve, who witnessed both the earthly Jesus and the post-resurrection appearances, was unique.[44] In fact, according to the Lukan paradigm, these appearances only lasted forty days, after which Christ ascended to heaven and sent the Spirit to the apostles who, on this basis, possessed unique religious authority (Acts 1:3; 2:4). Pagels concludes that for Irenaeus, access to

[42] Irenaeus lists the episcopal succession of the church of Rome, but he also mentions other apostolic churches to which appeal can be made for right belief, including those in Smyrna and Ephesus associated with John and Paul.

[43] Elaine H. Pagels, "Visions, Appearances, and Apostolic Authority: Gnostic and Orthodox Traditions," *Gnosis: Festschrift für Hans Jonas* (Göttingen: Vandenhoeck & Ruprecht, 1978) 417. As noted above, caution needs to be exercised with regard to the drawing of clear lines of distinction between the Gnostics and the catholics. Clearly there is overlap. For example, the Gnostics to a greater or lesser extent claimed apostolic authority for their ideas, although Pagels points out the differences between various groups of Gnostics on this point (421). Furthermore, there are "Gnostic" ideas (such as the need for personal illumination) within the New Testament and patristic writings. But on the issue of historical versus existential modes of revelation there appear to have been differences between the two types of Christianity.

[44] Pagels, "Visions," 416. The problem of the lateness of Paul's apostolic call and his apparent lack of witness to the earthly Jesus is an obvious problem in this paradigm. In light of this, the Gnostic-catholic dispute over the appropriation of Paul is somewhat understandable.

God and religious truth is dependent upon "the mediation of pres-byters and bishops, whose legitimacy was established 'from the begin-ning' through apostolic succession." Gnostics, on the other hand, claim immediate and direct access to the "source of revelation."[45]

The Nag Hammadi *Apocalypse of Peter* provides us with evidence that some late-second-century Gnostics believed the episcopal office was being abused by catholics who had failed to remain faithful to true Gnostic Christian beliefs.[46] *Apoc. Pet.* promotes Gnostic spirituality in the form of a vision of the spiritual Christ to Peter. Peter is commanded to become perfect in knowledge so that he might be the "beginning for the remnant whom [Christ has] summoned to knowledge," that is, the founder of the Christian Gnostic community (71.15-21). This knowledge is given to the elect through Christ and cannot be found in "the prophets" [i.e., the ancient Scriptures] (70.20–71.9). The "blindness" of those who crucified Jesus extends to those who will "accept our teaching in the beginning [but] will turn away" from the truth, that is, the catholics (72.5-12; 73.12-27). They turn away because they are loyal to "the father of their error" (73.27) who is presumably the God of the Old Testament "prophets." As the treatise continues, various opponents are condemned, apparently both Gnostic and catholic. These do not understand mysteries although they "speak of these things which they do not understand" and "have not been saved" because of their ignorance (76.27–77.10). Eventually we come to a rather clear denunciation of the developing catholic episcopacy. The author of *Apoc. Pet.* declares, "And there will be others of those who are outside our number who name themselves 'bishop' *(episcopos)* and also 'deacons,' as if they have received their au-thority from God. . . . Those people are dry canals" (79.22-31). In the apocalyptic vision Peter laments before Christ that these will be be-lieved "when they speak [Christ's name]" and will mislead multitudes, resulting in condemnation. Christ responds by assuring Peter that these leaders will only rule over "the little ones" (apparently the "true" Gnostic Christians) for a time, after which roles will be reversed and the little ones will rule over "those who are their rulers" (79.32–80.16). The "root of their error" will be pulled out and the impudence of the bishops and deacons will be exposed (80.17-21). Apparently the author of *Apoc. Pet.* had resigned himself to the improbability of reversing the

---

[45] Ibid., 429–30.

[46] This tractate is unrelated to the *Apocalypse of Peter* mentioned by the Church Fathers and now extant in Ethiopic. See Michel Desjardins, "Introduction to VII,3: Apocalypse of Peter," *The Coptic Gnostic Library: Nag Hammadi Codex VII*, ed. B. Pearson (Leiden: E. J. Brill, 1996) 201. Desjardins argues for a date of composition somewhere between 150 and 250 C.E. A late-second-century date seems likely to me.

ascendancy of the episcopacy, for he declares that "such persons shall remain unchanged" (80.22-23). Perkins concludes that the author of *Apoc. Pet.* presents himself as guardian of the tradition that has been distorted by the "heretical opinions" of the catholic officials.[47] Desjardins concludes from his analysis of *Apoc. Pet.* that "[anti-Christian] polemic was as much a feature of early Christianity as anti-Judaism."[48] In the case of this Gnostic author and his community, both the catholic Old Testament and the episcopal office (or at least those occupying it) were illegitimate authorities. Neither offered the true knowledge that comes directly from Christ.

All of this is crucial to a clear understanding of the use of Acts in Irenaeus' writings. First, in light of the context of the episcopal hermeneutical claims, Irenaeus' use of Acts to argue for the unity of the canon enables him to argue that *all* of the biblical witnesses testify to his "rule of faith," contrary to the Gnostic systems of thought that he opposes. Second, although his argument concerning the apostolic succession is not based upon Acts primarily (contrary to his "unity" argument), he is able to use Acts not only to argue for the unity of the developing canon, but also to support the doctrine of the succession. So, as will become clear in what follows, Irenaeus uses Acts to argue simultaneously for the unity of the developing canon and the legitimacy of the episcopacy. Although the former represents the major thrust of his use of Acts, the latter use serves to create the impression in the reader that according to Acts the entire canon is not only a unified witness, but a unified witness to Irenaeus' (primitive) trinitarian theology which had been preserved through the apostolic succession.

Irenaeus begins his biblical case by arguing that the apostles were granted "perfect knowledge" by the Holy Spirit beginning on the day of Pentecost as documented in Acts 2. This assertion is made in opposition to the claim of some Gnostics that the apostles had preached before perfect knowledge had been given. He declares,

> . . . it is unlawful to assert that they preached before they possessed "perfect knowledge," as some do even venture to say, boasting themselves as improvers of the apostles. For, after our Lord rose from the dead, [the apostles] were invested with power from on high when the Holy Spirit came down [upon them], were filled from all [his gifts], and had perfect knowledge: they departed . . . preaching the glad tidings . . . (3.1.1).[49]

[47] Perkins, *Gnosticism*, 178.

[48] Desjardins, "Apocalypse," 211–12.

[49] In 3.18.3 Irenaeus states that Christ was anointed by the Spirit "who is the unction" and that the Word declared by Isaiah, "'The Spirit of the Lord is upon me,

This argument is significant both in its content and in its place within Book 3. First, Irenaeus is establishing the "perfect knowledge" and authority of *all* the apostles as a result of the work of the Spirit. Second, this argument from Acts is used before he defends and uses the Gospels, Acts, and epistles generally to refute his opponents. In other words, the experience of Pentecost is historically and theologically foundational for Irenaeus and it is documented only in the book of Acts. Here we catch a glimpse of the canonically foundational nature of Acts for Irenaeus.

Throughout 3.12, Irenaeus uses Acts extensively in refuting the doctrines of his opponents. After opening chapter 12 with a recapitulation of the apostolic replacement of Judas Iscariot (Acts 1) according to the Scripture "which the Holy [Spirit], by the mouth of David, spake before concerning Judas," Irenaeus immediately reinforces the foundational nature of Acts 2 for his case by stating, "[When] the Holy [Spirit] had descended upon the disciples . . . Peter said . . . that this was what had been spoken by the prophet." He concludes from this that the same God who had promised by the prophet that He would send His Spirit upon the human race did in fact send the Spirit. Irenaeus notes that it is by the announcement of Peter in Acts that he knows this. Furthermore, he asserts that the apostles did not preach another God, but "the same God the Father . . . ; they exhorted them out of the prophets." According to Irenaeus, the apostles receive the same Holy Spirit as the one predicted by the Old Testament (specifically the prophet Joel). The result is the proclamation of the God of the Old Testament by the apostles as a part of the Gospel of Christ, and the linking of the oracles of the Old Testament prophets with the kerygma of the apostles—and Acts is the basis for this claim.

Irenaeus continues to argue from the book of Acts for the unity of the preaching of all the apostles. He notes that "Peter, together with John, preached to them [i.e., the multitude] this plain message of glad tidings." Acts demonstrates for Irenaeus the unity of the Jerusalem church, which "lifted up the voice to God with one accord." It is for

---

because He hath anointed me' pointing out both the anointing Father, the anointed Son, and the unction, which is the Spirit." An interesting and relevant parallel is found in 1 John 2:20 where the received text reads, "But you have an anointing from the Holy One, and you know all things" (NKJV). Verse 27 reads, "But the anointing which you have received from Him abides in you, and you do not need that anyone teach you; but as the same anointing teaches you concerning all things and is true, and is not a lie, and just as it has taught you, you will abide in Him" (NKJV). This is interesting testimony to the early Christian pneumatological doctrine of "perfect knowledge."

him the church from which every church had its origin and which manifested "the voices of the apostles . . . the truly perfect, who, after the assumption of the Lord, were perfected by the Spirit." Furthermore, when Peter speaks, he speaks as a representative of all the apostles and the Jerusalem church. Irenaeus claims that from the words of Peter in Acts we can understand what "the apostles" used to preach, the nature of their preaching, and their doctrine of God.

This representation of Peter and the rest of the apostles differs from that of most second-century Gnostics. Different Gnostic groups variously exalted and disparaged individual apostles. Desjardins notes, for example, that while anti-Petrine tendencies can be found within certain Gnostic groups (especially those which elevated James, Paul, and Thomas), others—like the anonymous author of the *Apocalypse of Peter* mentioned above—elevated Peter alone as the initial recipient of gnosis.[50] But in Irenaeus there is the attempt to use Acts as a means of placing all the apostles on an equal footing. Furthermore, while the Peter of *Apoc. Pet.* partly resembles the Peter of the Gospels, he is "not the Peter depicted in the other NT books . . . especially [the Peter of] Acts."[51] Desjardins notes that while the Peter of Acts is a "powerful and respected leader" after the descent of the Spirit at Pentecost, the Peter of the *Apocalypse* is never portrayed as anything but fearful and powerless (in spite of his gnosis).[52] He is commanded to be courageous until the parousia when he will be exalted (84.6-11). This may be evidence of the progressive dominance of the catholics on at least one Gnostic group. That is, for the catholics who are growing in power, Peter is a powerful forebear; for the increasingly marginalized community of *Apoc. Pet.*, Peter is a politically powerless but spiritually correct progenitor.[53]

After briefly arguing from the preaching of Philip, Irenaeus continues his case by arguing from Acts that Paul was in agreement with the Jerusalem church and the Twelve in his doctrine. He asserts that Paul also preached God as the Creator of the world. Then Irenaeus boldly declares that from the book of Acts (which he here calls "the very words and acts of the apostles"[54]) one can learn that "the whole range

[50] Desjardins, "Apocalypse," 207–08.

[51] Ibid., 204.

[52] Ibid.

[53] Some Gnostics appropriated a very different Peter, one whose power over both the community and his enemies was unmatched. See chapter 3 below.

[54] Irenaeus also refers to Acts as "the doctrine of the apostles" (3.14.4) and "the acts and the doctrine of the apostles" (3.15.1). For an interesting analysis of the significance of the title of Acts (The Acts of the Apostles) given to it by the "canonizing community," see R. W. Wall, "The Acts of the Apostles in Canonical Context," Robert W. Wall and Eugene E. Lemcio, *The New Testament as Canon: A Reader in*

of the doctrine of the apostles proclaimed one and the same God" and that this God was the maker of all things and the Father of Christ.

Irenaeus then moves into a discussion of the apostolic council in Jerusalem (Acts 15) and the letter which it produced—a letter which for Irenaeus proves his point "in a still clearer light." He argues that here the whole Church convened and, based upon the arguments of Peter and James concerning the coming of the Spirit upon the Gentiles, decided that the conclusions of the council were supported by the words of the prophets. Irenaeus concludes that "it is evident that they (i.e., the apostles) did not teach the existence of another Father, but gave the new covenant of liberty to those who had lately believed in God by the Holy Spirit." Furthermore, he asserts that the entire discussion of the issue of circumcision demonstrates that the apostles "had no idea of another god." In other words, Irenaeus is arguing for the oneness of God and the unity of the covenants based upon the unified apostolic affirmation of the divine origin of the Mosaic Law *and* the decision not to require the Gentiles to obey it. This decision, he argues, was based upon the prophetic prediction of the salvation of the Gentiles and the divine approval of the faith of the Gentile believers demonstrated by the outpouring of the Spirit upon them. Therefore, the God of ancient Israel, the Hebrew prophets, and all the apostles *agree* that the Gentiles are not bound to the law because of the evidence of the Spirit manifested in the Gentile believers. And it is the book of Acts which provides this argumentation for Irenaeus by linking these authorities.

In his use of the four Gospels, Irenaeus makes some highly significant and relevant statements regarding the Spirit, Scripture, and the rule of faith. In his famous passage on the necessity of four Gospels, he states that Christ gave the Church the Gospel "under four aspects, but bound together by one Spirit" (3.11.8). Here, the unity of the teaching of the apostles, which Irenaeus argues is the result of the Spirit's ministry, is extended explicitly to written texts.[55] Furthermore, Irenaeus asserts that the four Gospels "have all declared to us that there is one God, Creator of heaven and earth, announced by the law and the prophets;

Canonical Criticism (Sheffield: JSOT Press, 1992) 123–28. Wall argues that the word "Acts" places the text in the acts genre, a Hellenistic genre that emphasizes the supernatural powers of the story's hero(es). The phrase "of the apostles" identifies the entire group of apostles as the catholic community's predecessors vis-à-vis the claims of rivals like the Gnostics.

[55] This is a specific manifestation of a more general patristic pneumatology which Irenaeus shares—a theology in which the Spirit is the ultimate unifier. In this theological paradigm, the Spirit unifies believers to one another and to God. See 3.17.2.

and one Christ, the Son of God" (3.1.2). This simple binitarian theological summary represents the heart of the patristic rule of faith and, for Irenaeus, each gospel testifies to it.

The Muratorian Canon (ca. 200 C.E.) contains a very similar and potentially puzzling statement if not seen in this same historical and polemical context. The author states,

> Though various rudiments are taught in the several Gospel books, yet that matters nothing for the faith of believers, since by the one guiding Spirit everything is declared in all: concerning the birth, concerning the passion, concerning the resurrection, concerning the intercourse with his disciples and concerning his two comings, the first despised in humility, which has come to pass, the second glorious in royal power, which is yet to come.[56]

How can *everything* be declared in *all* the Gospels? How, for example, is Christ's birth declared in Mark? As the argumentation of Irenaeus indicates, the biblical documents are each seen as witnesses to the rule of faith, and because each author possesses "perfect knowledge" by the indwelling Holy Spirit, each "declares" the same rule even if the details vary. All of this is based on a reading of Acts 2 as foundational.[57]

Finally, Irenaeus argues for his doctrine from the New Testament epistles. Most of his argumentation here is irrelevant to our investigation of the canonical function of Acts. However, he makes two statements which have profound consequences in this regard. The first is found in 3.12.9 in the middle of his argumentation from Acts. After arguing for the unity of the teaching of Paul and that of the Jerusalem church from the account of Paul's sermon at Lystra (Acts 14), Irenaeus declares that "all [Paul's] Epistles are consonant to these declarations." Then in 3.13.3, after making a chronological argument from Galatians 2, Irenaeus declares that anyone who ascertains the time of Paul's journey to Jerusalem from the book of Acts will find that Paul's own statements concerning this are in agreement with those in Acts. Therefore, he concludes, the testimony of Paul is identical with the testimony of Luke concerning the apostles. The point here is not that Irenaeus overlooks the difficult chronological questions raised by a comparison of Acts with the Pauline epistles (especially Galatians)—something which he clearly does—but rather that: (1) the teaching of Paul in his

---

[56] Taken from the translation in Gamble, *NT Canon,* 93.

[57] For an interesting discussion of the unity of Scripture as primarily the unity of the divine message and the religious worldview, rather than the unity of a book (for both Jews and Christians), see Wilfred C. Smith, *What Is Scripture? A Comparative Approach* (Minneapolis: Fortress Press, 1993) 21–44.

epistles is, for Irenaeus, linked to his teaching in Acts; and (2) Acts seems to provide the backdrop against which the epistles must be understood. Here we begin to see the patristic concept of the epistles as extensions of the apostolic preaching in Acts, something that will be reinforced as this study continues.

I conclude this analysis of Irenaeus' use of Acts as a canonical unifier with an observation from 3.21.2-4 wherein Irenaeus defends the Septuagint (LXX). After arguing that the LXX is the inspired and divinely preserved version of the Old Testament, Irenaeus declares that the teaching of the apostles agrees with this translation, and that both the Jerusalem apostles and Paul—as well as their followers—declared the prophecies just as the translators of the Septuagint had recorded them. What forms the basis of Irenaeus' certainty that the declarations of the (translated) prophets and those of the apostles were in harmony with each other? He declares that "the one and the same Spirit of God" who proclaimed by the prophets also gave a true interpretation of the prophecies to the elders who translated the text and did himself announce through the apostles that the fullness of the times had arrived. So for Irenaeus, the Spirit—whose coming and unifying ministry are documented by the book of Acts—unites the original (Hebrew) utterances of the prophets, the translation of those utterances in the LXX, and the teachings (both oral and written) of the apostles.[58]

Thus far, all of the references to Acts which I have examined have involved Irenaeus' attempt to argue for a unified developing canon. But there is one more which is deserving of attention, due both to its nature and to its place within Irenaeus' argument. Near the end of his argumentation from Acts, Irenaeus makes reference to Acts 20:25-30 in an attempt to demonstrate the public nature of theological truth, in contrast to the Gnostic emphasis on private revelation. Acts 20:25-30 is part of a larger narrative unit in Acts which begins in 18:18 and ends in 20:38. This unit tells the story of Paul's encounter with the Ephesians. According to the text of Acts, Paul discovered some disciples of John

---

[58] Patterson, in analyzing the canonical contributions of Irenaeus, concludes that "it is quite true that Irenaeus' work has the effect of giving a body of Christian scriptures a unity and significance not before ascribed [sic] to them" and that his reliance on Acts for its account of the gift of the Spirit at Pentecost "gives support to the notion of the unity and continuity of the Apostolic preaching." See L. G. Patterson, "Irenaeus and the Valentinians: The Emergence of a Christian Scriptures," *Studia Patristica* 18 (1989) 191, 205, 206. For a description of Irenaeus' broader pneumatology, in which the Spirit is responsible for the "beauty, form, and order of the cosmos," see Thomas F. Torrance, "Kerygmatic Proclamation of the Gospel: The Demonstration of Apostolic Preaching of Irenaios of Lyons," *The Greek Orthodox Theological Review* 37/1-2 (1992) 117–19.

the Baptist in Ephesus who had known the baptism of John, but not that of Christ. After hearing the gospel, they were baptized in the name of Jesus, and, after Paul laid his hands on them, they received the Holy Spirit. Later in the text, after Paul has left and journeyed elsewhere, he is en route to Jerusalem and stops in Miletus. From there he calls for the Ephesian church leaders, who come to him and hear his final word of exhortation. Paul declares to them that the Holy Spirit has made them "bishops" *(episcopous)* over the church and that they are to take heed to their ministry because false teachers would arise from both within and without the church and would seek to draw disciples unto themselves.

Irenaeus does two interesting things with this text. First, he claims that bishops and elders came to Paul from Ephesus *and* from other surrounding cities, even though the text of Acts says nothing of any churches or elders besides those in Ephesus. This catholic reading gives the impression that Paul was sanctioning "bishops" from a number of Asian churches. Second, Irenaeus emphasizes Paul's claim that he had not failed to declare to them the entire "counsel of God." Thus, Irenaeus argues, the apostles declared everything to all. The implication here is that Acts 20 supports his claim that the bishops of the apostolic churches possess the whole truth. The reader is given the impression that Acts not only unifies the canonical witnesses, but that this unified canonical testimony supports the rule of faith as preserved through the apostolic succession—that (primitive) trinitarian theology which Irenaeus claims is taught in all the churches of the apostles. The text of Acts provides a basis for this claim because as Childs notes, in Acts 20 the Lukan Paul "addresses the future needs of the Christian church."[59]

So what we have with Irenaeus is the establishment of the episcopal hermeneutical claim primarily by means of historical argument (apart from the text of Scripture). He follows with the establishment of the unity of the developing canon based upon the text of Acts, and then reinforces the original hermeneutical claim with the text of Acts 18–20. This latter text provided him with the necessary paradigm for this reinforcement; and, as we will see below, it seems to have become increasingly useful for the patristic episcopal claim as time went on.

The Use of Acts in the Polemics of Tertullian

Tertullian of Carthage in North Africa was born into a pagan family around the year 155 C.E.[60] He gained a reputation as an expert lawyer in

---

[59] Brevard S. Childs, *The New Testament as Canon: An Introduction*, 2nd ed. (Valley Forge, Pa.: Trinity Press International, 1994) 233.

[60] Biographical information taken from Quasten, *Patrology*, Vol. 2, 246–81.

Rome and after his conversion to Christianity (ca. 193 C.E.) Tertullian applied his legal modes of thought to the exposition and defense of the faith. His literary activity took place between 195 and 220 C.E. Around the year 207 C.E. he became a Montanist, apparently as a result of his perception of the moral laxity of certain catholic bishops. It seems that Tertullian never really left the Church; rather, he appears to have modified his perspectives by incorporating Montanist insights into his theology. His works were foundational for Western Christianity and a number of his terms became a part of the Church's theological vocabulary. Included among the many literary works of his that have survived are *The Prescription of Heretics* and *Against Marcion* wherein he polemicizes against his theological opponents, and *On Baptism*, the only pre-Nicene treatise on Christian baptism to have survived.

As is the case with Irenaeus, Tertullian periodically articulates the outline of the rule of faith, sometimes in a binitarian form, and sometimes in a trinitarian one. In its standard trinitarian form, the rule for Tertullian is the belief in one God, the Father, who created all that is, and in one Lord, Jesus Christ, who was born of a virgin, was crucified, buried, and raised from the dead for human salvation, and who will return in judgment at the end of time, and in the Holy Spirit who provides believers with divine guidance. Like Irenaeus, Tertullian maintains that the rule of faith was given by Christ to the apostles, and by the apostles to the churches that they founded. The bishops in these churches had preserved the rule since the time of the apostles, and by recourse to these churches one could determine Christian truth. To a large extent it was the doctrinal and canonical work of Marcion which provided Tertullian with his primary polemical context.

Tertullian presents a radical version of the argument of Irenaeus with regard to hermeneutical authority. Because the apostles taught the entire rule to the churches and this rule is both public and well known, the rule itself not only comprises truth but provides the definite boundaries within which one can legitimately seek knowledge, determine the biblical canon, and interpret that canon. Tertullian acknowledges with his Gnostic opponents that believers must seek knowledge, but he asks, "[Where] ought our search to be made?" (*Prescr.* 12). After denying that truth can be found "amongst the heretics," he argues that believers should seek "in that which is [their] own, and concerning that which is [their] own"—that is, within the catholic rule of faith. He argues that even the woman of Luke 15 sought for her lost coin "within her own house" (*Prescr.* 12).

This may all sound self-evident to the reader who considers only the catholic perspective, but the Gnostics were making the same kinds of arguments. The Nag Hammadi *Testimony of Truth* describes the Gnostic

Christian mind as "the father of truth," wherein is revealed Gnostic doctrines like "the unbegotten aeons" and spiritual "light" and "power" (43.25-31). Here the Gnostic mind provides the "boundaries" within which the true believer should seek for knowledge and truth. Furthermore, although the author acknowledges that the Gnostic does, in fact, speak of these things when appropriate, he makes it clear to his readers that because the one who has received Gnostic enlightenment has ceased seeking for truth since he has already found it, he often refuses to engage in disputations with catholics but chooses, rather, to remain silent. He withdraws from the external world, "having ceased from loquacity and disputations" (68.27-29). He rejects these things, choosing to endure the nonsense of "the whole place" and the "evil things" around him, being patient with everyone and making himself "equal" to everyone even as he "separates himself from them" (44.3-16).[61] It is in the context of these kinds of Gnostic claims and strategies that Tertullian makes his case. Both sides were attempting to portray their religious paradigms as self-evidently true.

Tertullian applies his legal knowledge and experience to the issue of canon and its interpretation by employing the juristic principle of the prescription. The prescription was the barring of a case from being heard in court. It is not the presentation of an argument per se but the claim that a given case is not suited for presentation in court. Tertullian's *Prescription Against Heretics* is just such a prescription, but one presented in an ecclesiastical context rather than in a juridical one. Tertullian argues that in principle the "heretics" have no right to interpret the Scriptures because the Scriptures do not belong to them. They have no "title to the privilege" (*Prescr.* 15). When a believer argues with a heretic, three things happen, according to Tertullian: the strong in faith are wearied, the weak are mislead, and those in the middle—the waverers—are confused (15). These kinds of interpretive debates inevitably end up in gridlock and no one profits from them (18). For Tertullian, the real issue at stake here is the *ownership* of "the faith to which the Scriptures belong" (19). He asks, "From what and through whom, and when and to whom, has been handed down that rule, by which men become Christians?" (19). Then he makes one of the most significant statements in all of his writings with regard to the issue of canon. He asserts, "[Wherever] it shall be manifest that the true Christian rule

---

[61] Irenaeus declares that this Gnostic propensity toward silence is related to their doctrine of divine ineffability. Furthermore, he says, they base this principle on the example of Jesus in Matthew 21:23-27. Here the gospel writer records the refusal of Jesus to answer a Pharisaic question, a refusal which, for the Gnostics, shows "the unutterable nature of the Father" (*Adv. Haer.* 1.20.2).

and faith shall be, there will likewise be the true Scriptures and exposi-
tions thereof, and all the Christian traditions" (19). This statement reveals much about Tertullian's conception of Scripture. For him, one
need only determine which churches possess the true apostolic teaching, for wherever this is found will be found the true Scriptures (i.e.,
the texts which ought to be considered canonical) and the proper interpretation of those Scriptures.

Tertullian's effort here to undergird the authority of his developing
canon and his interpretation of those Scriptures is a part of the continuing late-second- and early-third-century attempts by various Christian
groups to define Christian "orthodoxy." The Marcionite canon and interpretation of canon provided much of Tertullian's impetus, but this
move on the part of Marcion was a part of the larger Gnostic critique of
developing catholicism in its various aspects. The debate over the authority of Scripture in the Church was not yet resolved. The catholics
and Gnostics accused each other of error in regard to both the nature of
religious textual authority and the proper ways of reading those texts.
The Testimony of Truth presents the kind of theological and bibliological
challenge that Tertullian is attempting to overcome. The Gnostic author
of *Testim. Truth* accuses the catholics of "great blindness" in their reading of the Old Testament (48.2-4). The dispute between the catholics
and the Gnostics over the nature and meaning of the book of Genesis
was at the heart of the larger debate over religious truth and authority
during this time, primarily because of its creation accounts. As described above, the basic difference in point of departure for the two
groups centered on the nature of the Creator. *Testim. Truth* provides a
fascinating example of the kind of hermeneutic that some Gnostics applied to the Old Testament in order to demonstrate its invalidity as an
authoritative corpus for the Christian community. In this case, the
author interprets the account of the Edenic test in Genesis 3. Pearson
observes that this "gnostic midrash" on the serpent of Genesis 3 is
"[one] of the most interesting sections of *Testim. Truth*."[62] The author
identifies the serpent as the wise one who offers humanity the knowledge of good and evil, and "God" (the creator) as the envious one who
refuses to share this knowledge with Adam and who demonstrates his
lack of omniscience by asking the question of Adam's whereabouts
(45.23–47.23). Furthermore, the creator-god "has shown himself to be a
malicious envier" by casting Adam out of the garden so that he (Adam)
might not live forever. "What kind of God is this?" the author asks
(47.28–48.1). He then proceeds to unite several other texts and traditions in an effort to demonstrate the superiority of the serpent. The rod

[62] Pearson, "Testimony," 106.

of Moses turned into a serpent which swallowed up the serpents of the magicians (Exod 7), and Moses hung the bronze serpent on a pole to deliver the people (Num 21). This serpent is Christ who saves those who believe in him (John 3). The failure of the catholics to make these connections reveals their failure to understand Christ spiritually (48.19–50.3).

The Gnostics represented by *Testim. Truth* understand truth and error in the opposite way that the catholics do. This alternative way of viewing reality provides the polemical context for Tertullian's claim that wherever his "rule of faith" is found, there will be the true Scriptures and the true interpretations of those Scriptures. Tertullian proceeds by arguing that the churches which the apostles founded all hold to the same rule of faith and hold "peaceful communion" with one another (20). He even claims that the only way to know what Christ really taught is to have recourse to the churches founded by the apostles. All doctrine that is in agreement with these churches is true (21) and it is inconceivable to him that so many churches could have gone astray into the same "error" as the "heretics" claim (27).

All of this is crucial for a sound understanding of Tertullian's use of Acts. As with Irenaeus, Tertullian has constructed a system in which he cannot lose. What Irenaeus states with modesty, however, Tertullian declares in extreme terms. His opponents have no case; there can be no legitimate debate because in principle the Scriptures are not theirs. And of course the interpretation of the text is known to Tertullian before the text is even examined.

Nevertheless, because there is so much proof from Scripture for his perspectives that no rebuttal will be possible, he announces that he will indulge his opponents and make his case from Scripture (22)! The use of Acts by Tertullian reinforces the work of Irenaeus in a number of ways. First, he strongly argues for a unified developing canon when, speaking of the Church, he says, "the law and the prophets she unites in one volume with the writings of evangelists and apostles, from which she drinks in her faith" (36). Second, he asserts that to know nothing in opposition to the rule of faith is to know all things (14), thus reinforcing the doctrine of "perfect knowledge" as described above. Third, he accuses Marcion of using Paul as an authority without any independent testimony to Paul's credentials. Tertullian insists that "the Acts of the Apostles . . . have handed down to me this career of Paul, which you must not refuse to accept" (*Adv. Marc.* 5.1). As Frend notes, Marcion had rejected Acts because from his point of view it "told the deeds of the disciples who had failed to understand Jesus' message" and was the work of Judaizers.[63] Furthermore, Tertullian here demon-

---

[63] Frend, *Early Church*, 56.

strates a vital principle of early Christian thought that is highly relevant to a discussion of the role of Acts in the canon. It has to do with the relationship between oral and written communication. He declares that that which the apostles preached can only be proven by recourse to the churches that they founded and which received their teaching first by oral proclamation and then later by their epistles (*Prescr.* 21). The point here is that for Tertullian, as for the Church Fathers in general, the writings of the apostles are extensions of their oral proclamations. Eusebius (ca. 320 C.E.) illustrates this well when he asserts that Matthew, who had at first preached to the Hebrews, when he was about to go to other peoples, committed his gospel to writing in his native tongue in order to compensate his hearers for the loss of his presence (*E.H.* 3.24.5-6). This is important because some interpreters have argued that Acts demonstrates the unity of the apostolic *preaching* for the Church Fathers, but not the unity of the New Testament canon.[64] But I would argue that if Acts demonstrates the unity of the apostles' preaching for the Fathers, it also unites the writings attributed to the apostles by being placed next to them in the canon. The early Christians did not make this kind of modern bifurcation between oral proclamation and written communication when the issue of apostolic authority was in view.[65] What mattered was the assurance that a tradition had come

---

[64] David W. Kuck, in his "The Use and Canonization of Acts in the Early Church" (STM Thesis, Yale University, 1975), argues this way. It is interesting to note that Paul (or an early Pauline disciple) makes no distinction—as far as authority is concerned—between his own oral and written modes of communication when in 2 Thessalonians 2:15 he urges the Thessalonians to "stand firm and hold fast to the traditions that you were taught by us, either by word of mouth or by our letter."

[65] As Barr insightfully asserts, "It no longer makes sense to speak of the authority of the Bible as if it meant the authority of the written documents, quite apart from the persons and lives that lie behind them. Authority must belong to both: certainly to the books, but not only to the books. Romans is authoritative because St. Paul is authoritative. . . ." Barr, *Holy Scripture,* 47–48. Most of the references to divine revelation in the Hebrew Bible—at least in the Nevi'im and Kethuvim—appear to portray orality as the original means of its dissemination, although references to the Law generally assume a written form, and, of course, the prophetic oracles themselves were eventually recorded. In the New Testament, the same trend can be observed: the teaching of Jesus and the apostles is at first disseminated orally and then in time assumes various written forms. When the Church Fathers appropriate apostolic tradition, however, there does not appear to be any qualitative distinction made between the two modes of communication. On the contrary, as evidence presented throughout this project will confirm, the two appear to carry equal weight as far as the issue of authority is concerned. As time goes on, the value of written tradition rises because it tends to be more conservative, thus producing a sense of "certainty" (cf. Luke 1:3-4).

from an apostle, whatever its form. As Keener notes, in antiquity, letters were considered "a surrogate for one's presence" and were supposed to reflect "the same character the person would display if present."[66]

But probably most significant in the writings of Tertullian is the connection between the outpouring of the Spirit on the apostles and the book of Acts. This is explicit in both the *Prescription* and *Against Marcion*. In the *Prescription* (22) he argues that Peter, James (of Zebedee), John, and the rest of the apostles did, in fact, "know all things," contrary to the claims of some Gnostics. Tertullian "knows" this because Jesus promised them the Spirit who would lead them into all truth and "assuredly He fulfilled His promise, since it is proved in the Acts of the Apostles that the Holy [Spirit] did come down." Furthermore, he asserts that those who reject the book of Acts can neither belong to the Holy Spirit, since they cannot prove that the Spirit had been given, nor can they show when the Church was first established. And in *Against Marcion* he similarly maintains that the promise of the Holy Spirit is shown to have been fulfilled "in no other document than the Acts of the Apostles" (5.2). But because of Acts, Tertullian believes that the promise of the Spirit which was proclaimed by the prophet Joel was "absolutely fulfilled" (5.8). So for Tertullian, no theological or canonical claims can be made without the book of Acts. It is inconceivable that he could have made this claim for any other biblical book, because, among other things, only Luke created a narrative account of the outpouring of the Spirit—a narrative which for Tertullian proves the theological credibility of the apostles and their unity with the prophets of ancient Israel.[67]

Not only does Tertullian establish the catholic hermeneutical prerogative on the basis of oral tradition and use Acts in an attempt to demonstrate a unified developing canon like Irenaeus, he also uses the Acts 18–20 narrative to reinforce the former. Although he does not explicitly link the passage to the authority of the catholic bishops, he does so indirectly. In his treatise, *On Baptism,* Tertullian uses Acts 19:1-7 to demonstrate the uniqueness of the baptism of Christ vis-à-vis the baptism of John the Baptist. While John's baptism simply provided a context for repentance, the baptism of Christ brings forgiveness and confers the Spirit (10). Tertullian then argues that although Christ did not himself baptize, his disciples were his representatives in their per-

---

[66] Craig S. Keener, *The IVP Bible Background Commentary: New Testament* (Downers Grove, Ill.: InterVarsity Press, 1993) 531.

[67] Ehrman notes that in Acts, the apostles and their churches stand in "complete harmony with one another." The value of Acts for the catholics is underscored by Ehrman's description of their view of truth. For them, truth is "unified, coherent, clear, ancient, and apostolic." See Ehrman, *Orthodox Corruption,* 6, 16.

formance of the rite (11). Next, he argues for the necessity of baptism (12-13) and answers the objection to baptism made by some Gnostics based upon Paul's statement in 1 Corinthians 1:17 that Christ had not sent him to baptize (14). Tertullian then establishes catholic baptism as the only legitimate form of the rite by discrediting the baptisms of "heretics" and Jews, and by upholding the authority of the bishops to both administer baptism and to authorize priests, deacons, and even the laity to do so (15-17).[68] Although Tertullian does not use Acts 19 directly to demonstrate all of this, it does appear to be a foundational text for him in this regard. For him, it demonstrates the qualitative difference between the baptisms of Christ and John and seems to provide a platform from which he can legitimize the baptisms performed by the catholic church in his day vis-à-vis all other forms of and objections to the rite.

As is the case with all early Christian polemics, Tertullian is addressing concerns raised by particular persons and groups, all of whom were striving to define "orthodoxy" during the late second and early third century. In *Testim. Truth* we have an example of one (or more) Gnostic's rejection of water baptism altogether during this time. The author describes the catholic[69] error concerning baptism in the following terms:

> Some enter the faith [by receiving a] baptism on the ground that they have [it] as a hope of salvation, which they call "the [seal]." They do not [know] that the [fathers of] the world are manifest in that place . . . (69.7-13).

The reference to the "fathers of the world" is apparently a description of the evil "archons" who rule over the material world. In the author's mind, the true God would not (and could not) use a material substance to produce a spiritual effect. He continues his polemic against catholic baptism by drawing support for his perspective from the gospel (possibly Johannine) tradition. He argues against baptism by declaring that Christ did not baptize his disciples (69.15-17), something which the author's opponents (like Tertullian) had to explain. The author of *Testim. Truth* then argues that if those who are baptized were "headed for life,"

---

[68] He had already discredited the baptisms performed by pagans earlier in the treatise.

[69] Pearson ("Anti-Heretical Warnings," 153) identifies this baptizing community as catholic, a conclusion that seems correct to me in light of the nature of the text and the concerns manifested throughout it—as well as the particular description of baptism here.

then the whole world would be saved! This is either a reference to the widespread practice of "baptisms" by numerous groups during the late second century (as Tertullian's polemic would seem to confirm), or a reference to the ease with which the world *could* be saved if baptism were efficacious.[70]

The author then argues for a different kind of "baptism": what he calls the "baptism of truth." He declares, "But the baptism of truth is something else; it is by renunciation of [the] world that it is found" (69.22-24). Those who merely claim to be renouncing the world (i.e., the catholics) are wicked and deceitful and are on their way to condemnation (69.24-32). Some catholics "fall away" to idol worship while others are indwelt by demons just as David and Solomon performed their kingly works "by means of the demons" (69.32–70.8). Although the reception of the Spirit on the part of the Gnostic by means of this "baptism of truth" is not explicitly affirmed here, the implication from other passages in the treatise would seem to support this. Earlier in the text the author describes the so-called baptism of Jesus as the end of "the dominion of carnal procreation" (30.29-30). When Jesus approached the Jordan, he declares, the waters of the Jordan turned back. John bore witness to the power which "came down upon the Jordan river" (30.24-28). The author of *Testim. Truth* then interprets the tradition allegorically, a phenomenon that characterizes Gnostic interpretation of Scripture and scriptural traditions in general. The Jordan river is the human body with all its senses and pleasures, especially those of a sexual nature. John the Baptist is the "archon of the womb," that is, a promoter of the fallen material realm (associated with the creator-god and the ancient Scriptures) from which the catholics have failed to free themselves. Victory over the passions comes to those who perfectly receive the "word of truth" from Christ (30.30–31.15). The descent of the Spirit upon Christ at his "baptism" confirms his birth from a virgin, a birth in which the Gnostic shares through the regeneration of the word of Christ (39.23–40.6). The implication seems to be that the Gnostic participates in the reception of the Spirit through the "baptism of truth" which the Gnostic, in effect, administers to himself by genuine renunciation of the world.

This dispute over baptism between catholics like Tertullian and Gnostics like the author of *Testim. Truth* during the late second and early third centuries is illustrative of the continuing efforts of these various interpreters of the Christian traditions to define "normative" Christianity. Tertullian has just begun to see the polemical potential of the Acts 18–20 narrative for grounding his view of the sacramental and

[70] Pearson, "Testimony," 190.

hermeneutical authority of the episcopacy in Scripture. As will become evident below, some of his post-Nicene successors will utilize the text in this way more fully.

Conclusion

In sum, this analysis of the use of Acts in the polemical writings of Irenaeus and Tertullian has demonstrated a particular function for the book—what I designate the "canonical function of Acts." After establishing their own hermeneutical prerogative and grounding their use of Acts in it, they both use Acts in an attempt to demonstrate the unity of those traditional prophetic and apostolic authorities who stand behind the developing canon in their "witness" to the patristic (trinitarian) rule of faith. For both Fathers, Acts demonstrates the unity of the biblical witnesses by means of the Holy Spirit. The prophets of Israel, Jesus, the Jerusalem apostles, and Paul—all of whom are represented by the respective sections of the developing canon—are all united in witness by their possession of the Spirit and the Spirit's influence on their proclamations, whether oral or written. By arguing for the unity of the biblical witnesses from the book of Acts, by linking that argument directly with the hermeneutical claim of the apostolic succession, and by using the Acts 18–20 narrative to reinforce that hermeneutical claim, these Fathers were able to harness Scripture and use it as a collection of texts that gave support to their own trinitarian theological systems. The work of the Gnostics—including Marcion, with his bifurcation of the God of Israel and the God of the Church and his limitation of the canon to a version of the Gospel of Luke and the Pauline epistles —accelerated the process of canonization in the Church and provided much of the context for the Church's polemical use of Acts. The result —namely the solidification of the heart of the biblical canon and the development of an accompanying hermeneutical office—as we will see, became a permanent part of catholic self-consciousness and identity, and created a permanent place in the catholic New Testament canon for the book of Acts.

There is evidence from Nag Hammadi that the use and canonization of Acts by the catholics during this time made an impact on at least one Gnostic community. The Gnostic *Letter of Peter to Philip (Ep. Pet. Phil.)* appears to betray a change in the Gnostic appropriation of apostolic authority. While during the second century it was common for Gnostics and catholics alike to base their arguments on traditions associated with one or a few particular apostles, the *Ep. Pet. Phil.* appears to be a third-century Gnostic response to the catholic use of the Lukan Acts to appropriate the traditions and texts of "all" the apostles.

The text of the *Letter* opens with an appeal by Peter, as a representative of all the apostles, to Philip, their "beloved brother" and "fellow apostle" (132.12-14). He tells Philip that they had received orders from the Lord and Savior of the whole world that they should come together to preach salvation. Peter then reminds Philip that not only was the latter separated from the other apostles when the orders came, but that he "did not desire [the apostles] to come together and to know how [they] should organize [themselves] in order that [they] might tell the good news" (133.1-5). Peter then very gently asks Philip to consent to the organizational meeting "according to the orders of our God Jesus" (133.6-8). Philip then returns to Peter and all the apostles "rejoicing with gladness."

This change on the part of Philip appears to reflect a change in the way our author and/or his community now perceived the nature of apostolic tradition. Whereas previously particular apostles were appropriated, now the entire group is presented as a unified foundational group. As the author of *Ep. Pet. Phil.* continues, the apostles gather together and pray for spiritual illumination and power. Christ appears, explaining to them the mysteries of Gnostic metaphysics and advising them to fight against the archons. In unison the apostles respond by asking how they will defeat the archons who are greater in power. Christ provides a specific answer: "[You] are to fight against them in this way: Come together and teach [salvation] in the world . . . [and] the Father will help you . . ." (137.22-29). Their *unified* testimony will overcome the powers of the evil creation. As the text continues, the apostles do indeed proceed to preach in such a manner. Peter is said to be "filled with a holy spirit," then, after a prayer for "a spirit of understanding," all the apostles are "filled with a holy spirit" (140.1-9). The apostles part company in order to preach but then come together again to greet and affirm each another by saying "Amen" to one another (140.11-15).

All of this betrays an influence on the part of the recently canonized Lukan Acts. As Meyer observes, the *Letter* "shares important features with part of the first (Petrine) section of the NT Acts of the Apostles."[71] He finds numerous parallels between the two documents, including similar scenes, themes, and terms.[72] Perkins argues that the framework of *Ep. Pet. Phil.* was formulated to address the kinds of arguments being put forth by catholics for the unity of the apostolic

[71] Marvin W. Meyer, "NHC VIII,2: The Letter of Peter to Philip: Introduction," *The Coptic Gnostic Library: Nag Hammadi Codex VIII*, ed. J. Sieber (Leiden: E. J. Brill, 1991) 229.

[72] Ibid.

teaching on the basis of the Acts of the Apostles. She attributes the catholic success in "pushing Gnostic authors to retreat" from the earlier second-century views of apostolic authority to the growing influence of the four-gospel canon and Acts.[73] My own reading of the *Letter* confirms this conclusion. One more parallel between Acts and the *Letter* should be noted, however. In the latter, the apostles gather together to address the question of suffering. Peter argues that the apostles must suffer because Christ suffered, whereupon Christ (in the form of a heavenly voice) confirms this (138.11-27). Not only does this reflect the probable influence of the Lukan Acts, it may also reflect the increasing marginalization which the third-century Gnostic Christians were experiencing vis-à-vis the catholic ecclesiastical network—a network dominated by the "bishops and deacons" who claimed to have "received their authority from God" but who were, from the point of view of some Gnostics, really "dry canals" (*Apoc. Pet.* 79.22-31).

It is no coincidence that Acts reached canonical status during the time of Irenaeus and Tertullian and that its canonical status was never seriously disputed after the beginning of the third century. Furthermore, it seems clear that its value for the catholics lay to a large extent in its unification of the biblical authorities and in its potential support for the catholic episcopal claim by means of its pneumatology. In Acts, the same Holy Spirit makes predictions through the prophets, fulfills those predictions in Jesus of Nazareth (who is also anointed with that Spirit), illuminates, unites, and empowers the Jerusalem apostles and Paul, and appoints episcopal successors to the apostles.[74] These qualities would also explain why Acts appears to have been a catholic document from the very beginning. From the surviving evidence, it does not appear that the Gnostics used the Lukan Acts as an authoritative document. The Nag Hammadi corpus contains possible allusions to Acts but manifests an apparent lack of direct or authoritative quotation. This is not surprising given the nature of the text of Acts and the implications of its content for the catholic arguments. With regard to Marcion, it is not difficult to see why he would not have held the document in

---

[73] Perkins, *Gnosticism*, 181.

[74] Interesting in this regard are the conclusions of Marsh who argues that in the writings of Irenaeus we see a revival of pneumatology. He writes, "this . . . rediscovery [of the Spirit] begins in the latter part of the second century and the man responsible for it was Irenaeus. The occasion which led to this new development was, I believe, the threat of Gnosticism. The Gnostic sects seem to have cashed in on the Church's neglect of the Spirit and to have attempted to appropriate the Spirit to themselves." See Thomas Marsh, "Holy Spirit in Early Christian Teaching," *The Irish Theological Quarterly* 45/2 (1978) 112.

high esteem. As Frend observes, "Acts which told the deeds of the disciples who had failed to understand Jesus' message . . . he rejected as the work of Judaizers."[75] Acts appears to have been written as a catholic document and utilized for catholic argumentation. It is my conviction that the connection between the canonicity of Acts and its ecclesiological implications is as significant in the writings of Irenaeus and Tertullian as the connection between Acts and the authority of Luke. That is, the intrinsic qualities of Acts contributed to its canonicity as much as the extrinsic association of its traditional author with the apostle Paul. The latter gave the document an *a priori* claim to authority and the former placed the document firmly into the developing canonical collection; indeed, into the very center of that collection.

[75] Frend, *Early Church*, 56.

Chapter 2

The Patristic Use of Acts:
Fourth Century

The foundational work done by Irenaeus and Tertullian with regard to the canonically-unifying function of Acts in the context of episcopal hermeneutical authority was incorporated into the works of subsequent Church Fathers. In this chapter I examine the works of two fourth-century writers—Cyril of Jerusalem and John Chrysostom—as testimony to this. These two fathers are representative of catholic thought during the century when the Christian Bible took its final form.[1] Furthermore, they provide the canon critic with two different genres for analysis: the catechism and the commentary.

The Use of Acts in the Catechism of Cyril

Cyril of Jerusalem became bishop of that city in 348 C.E.[2] His *Catechetical Lectures* provides a rather comprehensive overview of catholic doctrine during the mid to late fourth century. In his lecture on the Holy Spirit, Cyril finds great value in Acts as a source for pneumatology. In this context he asserts, "There is One Only Holy Ghost . . . He was in the Prophets, He was also in the Apostles in the New Testament" (16.3). He goes on to say,

[1] Irenaeus and Tertullian are crucial witnesses to the canon because it was during their time (and largely because of their work) that the heart of the canon was formed, a canon that included Acts. Likewise, because the fourth century produced the final form of the NT canon, it is crucial to examine the testimony of representative witnesses to the canonical function of Acts during this time; thus the choice of Cyril and Chrysostom, both of whom gave significant attention to Acts.

[2] Biographical information taken from Quasten, *Patrology*, vol. 3, 362–67.

> Let no one therefore separate the Old from the New Testament; let
> no one say that the Spirit in the former is one, and in the latter an-
> other; since thus he offends against the Holy [Spirit] Himself . . .
> let the Marcionites be silenced . . . we know the Holy [Spirit], who
> spake in the Prophets, and who on the day of Pentecost descended
> on the Apostles in the form of fiery tongues, here, in Jerusalem, in
> the Upper Church of the Apostles; for in all things the choicest
> privileges are with us (16.4).

Here Cyril seems to imply that Acts 2 is evidence that the two Testaments must be united into one canon. Furthermore, his specific denunciation of the Marcionites in this context provides testimony to the
continuing influence of the sect and its philosophy of canon in the century normally associated with the Arian controversy. As will become
evident, the polemical use of Acts against Marcion, inherited from the
earlier fathers, has become a part of Cyril's catholic self-consciousness
and his catechetical rhetoric.

   Throughout Lecture 16, Cyril adduces evidence from various biblical texts to support his general pneumatology, primarily from the Old
Testament. He ends by stating his intention to use the New Testament
in the next lecture. In fact, though, throughout Lecture 17 it is Acts
which functions as the primary text for his exposition, and the experience of Pentecost is central. Jackson is correct when she concludes that
the Pentecost episode is foundational for Cyril is his instruction on the
Holy Spirit.[3] Referring to the account of Jesus' breathing the Spirit on
the apostles in John 20, Cyril asserts that this episode bestowed divine
grace only partially because the apostles were not ready to receive it in
full measure. Cyril notes that Jesus instructs them to wait in Jerusalem
for the outpouring of the Spirit. Then he observes,

> So they were sitting, looking for the coming of the Holy [Spirit];
> and when the day of Pentecost was fully come, here, in this city of
> Jerusalem . . . the Comforter came down from heaven . . . He
> came down to clothe the Apostles with power . . . His power was
> in full perfection . . . so were they also baptized completely by the
> Holy [Spirit] (17.12-14).

He goes on to contrast the experience of the tower of Babel with the
experience of Pentecost and notes that at Pentecost "minds were re-

---

[3] Pamela Jackson, "Cyril of Jerusalem's Treatment of Scriptural Texts concerning the Holy Spirit," *Tradition: Studies in Ancient and Medieval History, Thought, and
Religion* 46 (1991) 1–31. For a more general analysis of Cyril's use of Scripture as a
collection of witnesses to the creed, see idem, "Cyril of Jerusalem's Use of Scripture
in Catechesis," *Theological Studies* 52 (1991) 431–50.

stored and united *(apokatastasis kai henōsis tōn gnōmōn)*,[4] because . . .
the self-same Spirit, continuing what He is, as He had often wrought in
Prophets, now manifested a new and marvellous work" (17.17-18).

After discussing Peter's Pentecostal sermon, Cyril then says that
many passages are still to come from the Acts of the Apostles in which
the grace of the Holy Spirit wrought mightily "in Peter and in all the
Apostles together"; many also from the catholic epistles and the epistles
of Paul. It is not altogether clear here whether he is claiming to be able
to demonstrate the united testimony of the apostles (as a result of the
Spirit's work) from the epistles as well as from Acts, or simply that the
epistles provide more grounds for a general pneumatology. While it
appears that the former is implied, *in fact* he only touches briefly on the
Pauline epistles and never uses the catholic epistles because "time
would fail" him if he did (17.34). What he does, instead, is continue to
use Acts to claim that "with this Holy Spirit Paul also had been filled
after his calling" and "in the power of the same Holy Spirit Peter also,
the chief of the Apostles and the bearer of the keys of the kingdom of
heaven," conducted his ministry. The reader gets the impression that
for Cyril, Acts is a sort of "mini-canon" by which he can demonstrate
the doctrine of all the apostles.[5]

But as with Irenaeus and Tertullian earlier, the hermeneutical authority which the catholic bishops claimed provides the context for and
presupposition behind Cyril's use of Acts as a canonical unifier. Scripture is a collection of witnesses to the rule of faith found in the catholic
Church. In Lecture 18, Cyril glosses the phrase "[We believe] in one
Holy Catholic Church" found in the Jerusalem creed. He argues that
the term "catholic" is crucial as a description of the network of churches
to which he belongs and which he believes preserves the truth and
alone has the power to regenerate humanity. It is catholic, he argues,
because it extends over all the world, it teaches universally and completely all the doctrine that humanity ought to know, it produces piety
in the whole human race, it removes sin, and it possesses every virtue
and spiritual gift (18.23). When one is traveling abroad, Cyril argues, it
is imperative to ask where the "catholic Church" is, not just where the
"Church" is, because some congregations are churches of "evil-doers"
—specifically the churches of the Marcionites and Manicheans (18.26).
This reference again to the Marcionites, and to the Manichaeans as
well, is, in my view, quite significant. One might expect him to condemn

---

[4] Literally, "reversal and union of the thoughts."

[5] The term "mini-canon" as a description of Acts was first suggested to me by
Vasiliki Limberis of Temple University in a discussion of my interpretation of the
use of Acts in the patristic period.

and warn his catechumens about Donatist and Arian churches since Donatism and Arianism were controversies specific to the fourth century, but he does not. This reference would seem to demonstrate both the continuing influence of Marcionism and that of the neo-Gnostic Manichaean movement on the one hand, and, on the other hand, the inextricable link between these kinds of opposition movements and the late-second/early-third-century catholic use of Acts to combat them.[6] Cyril here appropriates the Acts 18–20 narrative. He argues from Acts 19:41 that the term *ekklēsia* is insufficient to identify the Church of Christ, for here the term refers to an assembly of Ephesian idolaters. For this reason "the Faith" (i.e., catholic tradition) has "delivered to thee the Article, 'And in one Holy Catholic Church'" (18.26). The Acts 18–20 narrative has become the basis for identifying Cyril's network of churches as the one true Church possessing theological truth and hermeneutical authority by its (Acts') identification of the "Other"—that is, the churches of the "evil" Marcionites and Manichaeans.

In order to establish the sole legitimacy of the catholic Church, Cyril appropriates a number of canonical witnesses from both Testaments—something which his use of Acts enables him to do. He argues from Leviticus and Deuteronomy that the assembly of the congregation of Israel was the precursor of the Church. The Psalmist testifies to the Church when he gives thanks "in the great Congregation" and exhorts others to do the same. And because Israel rejected the Messiah, they were rejected by God, as David "prophesies" in Psalm 26, "I have hated the Congregation of evil doers." Cyril further argues that the same David prophesies of the "second Holy Church" (i.e., the catholic Church) when he declares in the same Psalm, "Lord, I have loved the beauty of Thine house" and "[in] the Congregations will I bless thee, O Lord." Malachi and Paul are then quoted for further support (18.24-25). Cyril concludes his lecture on ecclesiology by arguing that while the authority of earthly kings is limited to particular geographical locations, only the "Holy Catholic Church" extends its power "without limit over the whole world" (18.27). This exaltation of catholic authority is best understood in light of the competing theologies and assemblies of the Marcionites and Manichaeans. Both groups enjoyed success during the third and fourth centuries and were perceived by Cyril as very real threats to the catholic network.

For Cyril, the book of Acts unifies the canon, but the "unified" witness of Scripture is only understood in the context of the hermeneutical

---

[6] This is confirmed by Cyril's denunciation of the various "heretical" groups in Lecture 6 where the Marcionites and the Manicheans figure prominently in his polemics because of their theological dualism.

authority of the catholic Church. For Cyril, the Jews, Samaritans, pagans, Marcionites, Manichaeans, and others are misguided either in their failure to acknowledge certain writings as canonical or in their interpretation of those writings. He argues that the Greeks "receive not what is written" (i.e., fail to acknowledge the catholic canon) and must be refuted with reason alone (18.10). The Samaritans acknowledge part of the canon (the Pentateuch) but misinterpret even that which they acknowledge (18.11-13). Certain anonymous heretics acknowledge the Prophets as canonical but "have made ill use of [them]" through faulty interpretation (18.14). And of course, for Cyril, the Jews cannot be hermeneutically legitimate because of their rejection of Christ (18.25), and the Marcionites are just plain "evil" (18.26). But God has given to the catholics "wisdom and understanding" among numerous other virtues (18.27). For Cyril—as for Irenaeus and Tertullian before him—Acts unifies the canon and warns against "false" churches (i.e., non-catholic ones). He incorporates the work done by those before him in this regard, without any significant development of that work. This will change with the homiletics of Chrysostom.

John Chrysostom's Commentary on Acts

John Chrysostom was born into a wealthy Christian family in Antioch of Syria between 344 and 354 C.E.[7] As a young man he was trained in philosophy and rhetoric and at the age of eighteen took a particular interest in theology. He spent two years as an ascetic in study before being ordained as a priest in Antioch. In 398 he became bishop of Constantinople. Chrysostom established for himself the reputation of being the greatest orator of the patristic period.

In his *Commentary on the Acts of the Apostles,* John Chrysostom provides evidence of his understanding of the function of Acts within the Christian canon. Commenting on Acts 1–2, he declares, "so replete is [the book of Acts] with Christian wisdom and sound doctrine, especially in what is said concerning the Holy [Spirit]." He goes on to argue that great change took place in the apostles because of the outpouring of the Spirit upon them. Before Pentecost, he exclaims, the apostles were ignorant, fearful, and *divisive*. But after the Spirit was poured out upon them, they became humble and *united*. Regarding the tongues of fire seen at Pentecost, he says, "Cloven, for they were from one root; that you may learn, that it was an operation sent from the Comforter." He clearly understands this to be evidence that each one present partook of the same Spirit. In fact, he notes that Peter spoke for all twelve

---

[7] Biographical information taken from Quasten, *Patrology,* vol. 3, 424–45.

apostles in order that they might express themselves "through one common voice."

But the strongest evidence that Chrysostom regarded Acts as the unifier of the canon comes from his comments on Acts 15 (the Jerusalem council). He argues that what *Peter said* at the council regarding salvation by grace through faith agrees with what *Paul writes* in Romans: "The same that Paul says at large in the Epistle to the Romans, the same says Peter here." And with regard to Paul's doctrine in 1 Corinthians and Ephesians, Chrysostom declares, "Of all these the seeds lie in Peter's discourse." So for Chrysostom, the preaching of Peter in Acts is expanded in the epistles of Paul. In a similar manner Chrysostom argues in his comments on Acts 20:32 that what Paul does when *writing* an Epistle he also does when *speaking* in council. The unity of the apostolic oral proclamation in Acts is, for Chrysostom, extended throughout the writings of the New Testament. Furthermore, he argues that James "is not divided from [Peter and Paul] in opinion," that John and the other apostles could have spoken at the Jerusalem council but chose to hold their peace "so clean was their soul from love of glory," and that the decree "made in common" stood in agreement with the words of the Old Testament prophets. Chrysostom then makes a telling transition. Encouraging his readers/hearers not to be disheartened by heresy, he employs "speech in character" *(prosōpopoiia)*[8] and urges the theoretical "heathen" seeker of truth to find the true doctrine in the Scriptures. He maintains that "if any agree with the Scriptures, he is the Christian; if any fight against them, he is far from this rule." So for Chrysostom, the united apostolic witness of Acts is linked to the oracles of the Old Testament and extended throughout the writings of the New Testament. He reaches this conclusion from a reading of Acts 2 and 15. In this sense Acts functions for him as the unifier of the canon.[9]

This canonical function assigned by Chrysostom to Acts is strengthened by a contrast with Chrysostom's *Commentary on the Epistle of St. Paul the Apostle to the Galatians*. The comparison is interesting because

[8] "Speech-in-character" is a rhetorical device wherein the author creates a dialogue or debate with an imaginary or real interlocutor to illustrate his or her point. For a full discussion of this technique and its hermeneutical implications, see Stanley K. Stowers, *A Rereading of Romans: Justice, Jews, and Gentiles* (New Haven, Conn.: Yale University Press, 1994) esp. 16–21.

[9] As von Campenhausen notes, the "successors" of the apostles "remain bound by the original apostolic word and witness, which finds its definitive form in the New Testament canon. It was the latter which in a certain sense became the real heir of the apostles' authority." See Hans von Campenhausen, *Ecclesiastical Authority and Spiritual Power in the Church of the First Three Centuries*, trans. J. Baker (Stanford, N.J.: Stanford University Press, 1969) 23–24.

Paul does claim in this epistle that the "pillar" apostles (James, Peter, and John) gave him the "right hand of fellowship" (2:9). By this statement (and a few others in Galatians) Chrysostom is able to assert the unity of the apostolic preaching. For example, commenting on 2:2 he asserts, "the Apostles found no discrepancy in his preaching, but confirmed it." However, the ambiguity of Paul's relationship with the Jerusalem apostles reflected in Galatians is also clearly a problem for Chrysostom. In his comments on 1:1-3 he observes, "that this Epistle breathes an indignant spirit, is obvious to every one even on the first perusal." With regard to the question of the lateness of Paul's apostolic call (1:15-16), Chrysostom asserts that although he knows his hearers desire an answer, he cannot give it to them. They must beg God to reveal it to them. In his comments on 1:17 ("neither went I up to Jerusalem to them which were before me") Chrysostom must explain these words which seem to breathe "an arrogant spirit." In fact, though he argues for apostolic unity, he must go to great lengths throughout the commentary on chapters 1–2 to demonstrate this, even arguing that Paul's rebuke of Peter at Antioch was a prearranged charade which the apostles carried out for heuristic reasons, and admitting that "many, on a superficial reading of this part of the Epistle, suppose that Paul accused Peter of hypocrisy"—something which Chrysostom denies. It is evident that for the archbishop (and for the "many" who read the letter otherwise) Galatians could not function as the unifier of the canon, notwithstanding the scattered comments on the unity of the apostles which it contains.

But again, as with Irenaeus and Tertullian earlier, Chrysostom's use of Acts as a means of appropriating the entire canon as a collection of witnesses to catholic theology is intricately connected to his claims of episcopal authority. Nowhere is this seen more clearly than in his commentary on the Acts 18–20 narrative. Chrysostom calls attention to Paul's question in Acts 19:2, "Did you receive the Holy Spirit when you became believers?" He notes that Paul did not ask the disciples of John whether they had believed in Jesus, but, rather, whether they had received the Spirit. Chrysostom claims that Paul knew they had not in fact received the Spirit but wanted to confront them directly with the issue. The ensuing pages of commentary reveal that this issue is fundamental for the bishop. It is the baptism of Christ as continued in the catholic Church that provides the Church with its central identity. Chrysostom argues that this episode in Acts 19 demonstrates the inadequacy of John's baptism and the efficacy of catholic baptism for the reception of and participation in the Spirit. In fact, although the ministry of John the Baptist had long been appropriated by the Christians as a part of their salvation history, Chrysostom maintains that if all the Church knew was John's baptism there would be a lack of virtue and many false prophets. But through catholic baptism, the Church has received "remission of sins, sanctification, participation of the Spirit, adoption, eternal life" as well as the "abiding things": faith, hope, and love. Through the catholic sacraments, Christians partake of "the same spiritual food."

As Chrysostom continues his commentary on the Acts 18–20 narrative, the connection between the unifying function of Acts and the hermeneutical prerogative of the catholic bishops becomes clear. His comments on Acts 20:26-30 are especially telling. In this pericope Paul addresses the "bishops" *(episcopous)* from Ephesus who, according to the text, had been appointed as such by the Holy Spirit. Paul claims to have declared the entire "counsel *(tēn boulēn)* of God" to the "bishops" and is, therefore, innocent of the blood of all. Consequently, the "bishops" must use this deposit of revelation to guard both themselves and the church against the "savage wolves" who would arise from within the church and outside the church to draw disciples away from the truth. In Chrysostom's commentary on all of this, the text is appropriated in a telling way: Paul and the Ephesian "bishops" become Chrysostom and all the catholic bishops.[10] The latter are guilty of "murder" if they do not fulfill their divinely appointed role as overseers. Addressing the bishops in his audience, Chrysostom asserts, "See, it is from the Spirit ye have your ordination." There is no significant distinction made by the commentator between the "bishops" of Ephesus in the first century and the catholic bishops of the late fourth century. For Chrysostom, Paul's baptizing ministry conferred the Spirit, and this Spirit in turn appointed the bishops of the church. This process continued right up until Chrysostom's own day in the episcopal succession. When Paul reminds the Ephesian overseers that he had not ceased to warn them night and day with tears about the "heretics" (v. 31), Chrysostom urges his fellow-bishops that "this might well be said in our case also."[11] He bemoans the fact that his lay hearers fail to heed his clerical warnings against a number of vices like attending theatre, swearing, coveting, and complaining. This conscious identification of the fourth-

---

[10] Although Chrysostom obviously sees himself in the line of apostolic succession, he sometimes identifies himself as much with Paul as with the successors of Paul.

[11] Chrysostom does make secondary application here and elsewhere to the laity regarding their own responsibility to guard themselves. Furthermore, he periodically makes a distinction between Paul and himself as when he says, commenting on Acts 20:26 (where Paul claims to be innocent), "we dare not say [this], conscious as we are of numberless faults." But this is clearly a gesture of humility, not a lessening of the episcopal claim.

century bishops with the apostles and "bishops" in Acts is a specific manifestation of Chrysostom's general use of biblical history to teach moral and spiritual lessons to his hearers by means of participation in that history. As Wylie observes, for Chrysostom, the earliest Christians are not just saints to be admired and imitated, but ancestors who are organically linked to Christians of the following centuries. For him, "[the] apostles are the founders of the church that still thrives in [his] day. . . . The book of Acts tells the history of these founders."[12]

As the *Commentary* on Acts 20:26-31 comes to a conclusion, Chrysostom makes a fascinating move—one that serves to underscore the connection between his use of Acts as a canonically unifying document and his own episcopal claims: he appropriates other canonical witnesses (one Old and several New Testament texts), ending with the testimony of Paul—but this time from Paul's epistles. First, Moses prefigures the archbishop when he declares in Deuteronomy 3:26, "The Lord was angry with me on your account." Chrysostom likens the ministry of Moses to his own; there is continual grief and anguish experienced by both leaders in regard to the failure of their congregations. Then, Chrysostom leaps to the New Testament epistle to the Hebrews where it is said that the church leaders ought to be obeyed because they "watch over your souls and will give an account" (13:17). And finally, numerous phrases from Paul's epistles are either quoted or paraphrased to give rhetorical strength to Chrysostom's own episcopal claims.

Chrysostom has used the Acts 18–20 narrative as a justification for catholic sacramental and theological authority. The apostolic ministry of Paul conferred the Spirit and through the Spirit appointed apostolic successors. For Chrysostom, these successors continued to his own day in the persons of the bishops who both receive and confer the Spirit, and "guard" the Church by means of the entire (apostolic) "counsel" of God, just as the text of Acts describes. From here he can appropriate the authority of other biblical witnesses for his case because in his mind the text legitimizes his hermeneutical authority.[13]

---

[12] Amanda Berry Wylie, "The Exegesis of History in John Chrysostom's *Homilies on Acts*," *Biblical Hermeneutics in Historical Perspective*, ed. M. Burrows and P. Rorem (Grand Rapids, Mich.: Wm. B. Eerdmans Publishing Co., 1991) 68.

[13] The role of the Acts 18–20 narrative in the development and legitimation of episcopal hermeneutical authority may be significant beyond the paradigmatic nature of Paul's conferring of the Spirit and the Spirit's appointment of bishops. The fact that this occurs in Ephesus may be meaningful. E. Lemcio argues that Ephesus was the *Sitz im Leben* of the New Testament canon. That is, Ephesus was in one way or another associated in early church tradition with a number of apostles and apostolic associates, and with a number and a diversity of New Testament documents. Lemcio notes that Ephesus is referred to in the New Testament more than any other

So the book of Acts not only functions for Chrysostom as the unifying center of the canon, it also specifically legitimizes the episcopal structure of the catholic Church, thus enabling him (and the other bishops) to appropriate the entire biblical canon as a unified witness to catholic dogma. The pneumatology of Acts is central in both regards. The Spirit unites the biblical witnesses and appoints the catholic bishops as guardians and interpreters. Here, that which Irenaeus and Tertullian created in their disputes with various Gnostics in the late second and early third centuries is not simply incorporated; it is developed and made more explicit. That is, *they* used Acts primarily to argue for the unity of the developing canon, and secondarily to support the episcopal claim—a claim which was itself based primarily on (oral) historical arguments. But in the work of Chrysostom, the use of Acts 18–20 to support the episcopacy is much more substantial and begins to rival the use of Acts as a canonical unifier. Here, the function of Acts as a unifier and its function as support for the episcopacy are virtually inseparable.

It may be that the commentary genre itself partially explains this development. Irenaeus and Tertullian had not written commentaries on Acts; their use of Acts represents the selective use of portions of the text for polemical purposes. In dealing with the text in an orderly and relatively comprehensive manner, Chrysostom may have realized the full potential of the text to support the hermeneutical authority of the bishops. It is also likely, however, that the moral overtones of Paul's pronouncements in the Miletian speech were appealing to the moralizing archbishop and programmatically useful for him. Paul declares to

---

city except Jerusalem (17 times), that it is mentioned in six different New Testament documents (including Acts, 1 Corinthians, Ephesians [if the textual evidence is accepted], 1 Timothy, 2 Timothy, and Revelation), and that according to New Testament and patristic sources, it was visited by personages such as Paul, Luke, John, Apollos, Timothy, and Mark. He even proposes that Acts was written in Ephesus. His evidence includes similarities between the Gospel of Luke and the Synoptic-like traditions in the Gospel of John, and the attention devoted by Luke to Paul's Ephesian ministry—one that in the text of Acts lasts longer (3 years) than Paul's ministry anywhere else, including Rome, and one which is given a significant amount of textual space. Based on these and other kinds of evidences, Lemcio concludes that Ephesus was a kind of proto-catholic city, one that could embrace a diversity of persons, doctrines, and literary genres within certain limits, and the city that served as the matrix of the New Testament canon. His argument seems substantial to me and appears to give added significance to the Acts 18–20 narrative and the patristic use of that passage. See Eugene E. Lemcio, "Ephesus and the New Testament Canon," ed. R. Wall and E. Lemcio, *The New Tesament as Canon: A Reader in Canonical Criticism* (Sheffield: JSOT Press, 1992) 335–60.

the Ephesian "bishops" that *he* is "not responsible for the blood of any of [them]" and that *they* are to keep watch over the Church which Christ "purchased with his own blood"[14] (Acts 20:26, 28). As noted above, Chrysostom declares to the clergy in his audience that on the basis of this text they are guilty of "murder" if they do not fulfill their divinely appointed role as overseers of the Church. Furthermore, he exhorts them to consider "how precious the concern" for ecclesiastical leadership really is since Christ did not even spare his own blood for the Church. The "peril is about no small matters," he says.

Chrysostom's commentary on Acts represents fifty-five sermons which he preached in Constantinople around 400 C.E.[15] Soon after his consecration as patriarch there in 398, Chrysostom determined to reform the clergy whom he believed had become corrupt.[16] His campaign failed and his attacks on ecclesiastical and political leaders brought resentment and opposition from both quarters. Chrysostom spent his last days in exile. It was during this campaign, however, and probably in part because of it, that the full potential of the Acts 18–20 narrative to support the catholic concept of the episcopacy began to be realized. The well-known influence that Chrysostom's works had on subsequent leaders of the Church makes his use of Acts all the more significant.

---

[14] This latter phrase is taken from Chrysostom's text. Here the NRSV reads, "that he (God) obtained with the blood of his own Son." The difference is explained by a textual variant.

[15] Quasten, *Patrology*, vol. 3, 440.

[16] Ibid., 425; see also the discussion in W.H.C. Frend, *The Early Church: From the Beginnings to 461*, 3rd ed. (London: SCM Press Ltd., 1991) 210.

Chapter 3

The Patristic Use of Acts:
The Works of Bede as
Synthesis and Development

I conclude the presentation of patristic evidence for the twofold canonical function of Acts with an analysis of the commentaries of the late-seventh- and early-eighth-century English scholar, the Venerable Bede.[1] This analysis is relevant because of Bede's heavy use of the fathers,

---

[1] Unless otherwise noted, all quotations from Bede are taken from The Venerable Bede, *Commentary on the Acts of the Apostles*, trans. L. T. Martin (Kalamazoo, Mich.: Cistercian Publications, 1989), and *The Commentary on the Seven Catholic Epistles of Bede the Venerable*, trans. D. Hurst (Kalamazoo, Mich.: Cistercian Publications, 1985). Bede makes some interesting statements concerning the canon in general—statements that I have not found in recent works on the canon. (Scholarly analyses in general tend to deal with the patristic and modern periods, giving little or no attention to evidence from the medieval period.) For example, Bede explains the purpose of written Gospels thus: "the words and deeds of Christ were put together in written form . . . so that subsequent teachers in the church might be supplied with confidence and authority for preaching and writing about those things which they had not seen" (*Comm. on Acts*, 5). Also, he emphasizes the catholicizing tendency of the canonical process by stating repeatedly that the canonical writings are written to all Christians. For example, of Theophilus as recipient of the book of Acts he claims, "Theophilus means lover of God, or beloved of God. Therefore, anyone who is a lover of God may believe that this [work] was written for him, because the physician Luke wrote it in order that he [the reader] might find health for his soul" (ibid., 9). And he proposes a fascinating resolution of the knotty problem of Jude's quotation of an "apocryphal" work (1 Enoch) which he describes as "tainted by a lie." After acknowledging that a "number of people from the earliest times" had rejected Jude on account of this, he argues that it is considered canonical by the Church

and also because of the influence he exerted on those who came after him in the West. Hurst notes that Bede's reputation as a Scripture scholar, in fact, has generally been that of a "clever compiler of the insights of previous exegetes rather than that of a thinker of any originality."[2] Bede regularly draws from the works of Cyprian, Ambrose, Jerome, Augustine, and Gregory the Great, and occasionally from those of Didymus, Athanasius and John Chrysostom.[3] Furthermore, Bede is greatly concerned about the unity of Christian doctrine. Martin notes, "Bede frequently makes references to [ancient] heresies and heretics as well, showing . . . his sense of identification with the patristic church. . . ."[4]

Bede's works are witnesses not just to his own views, but also to his understanding of patristic doctrine. What do the works of Bede tell us about his and the Fathers' understanding of the canonical function of Acts? We begin with his commentary on Acts. In his comment on Acts 1:12, he notes that Christ sent the Holy Spirit, "by whose anointing we are taught all things," underscoring the early Christian belief that the Spirit grants "perfect knowledge." He goes on (1:26) to explain the monumental dispensational change which took place at Pentecost, arguing that the casting of lots was appropriate in decision-making only before the Spirit was given. Most significantly, in his discussion of 28:25-26, where Paul declares to the Jewish leaders in Rome that the Holy Spirit was right when he spoke through the prophet Isaiah, Bede declares:

> Nor indeed did Paul possess a different Holy Spirit, when he wrote these things about him, from the one which was in the prophets before the advent of the Lord. Rather [he wrote] about him whom he himself had shared in . . . Peter also, in the sermon in which he persuaded those who were present, said, "The scripture must be fulfilled which the Holy Spirit . . . declared before by the mouth of David concerning Judas." Thus he also showed that the same Spirit was at work in the prophets and in the apostles. These excerpts from the books of the blessed Didymus should have this place in our little work.

---

because of its "authority and age and usefulness" and because the "witness" that Jude takes from 1 Enoch is itself "not apocryphal and doubtful but outstanding because of its true light and light-giving truth" (*Comm. on Jude*, 249–50).

[2] D. Hurst, in *The Commentary on the Seven Catholic Epistles of Bede the Venerable*, xvi.

[3] Ibid., xvi, 98, 101; and *Comm. on Acts*, 195.

[4] L. T. Martin, in The Venerable Bede, *Commentary on the Acts of the Apostles*, xxiii.

For Bede, a commentary on Acts is the appropriate place to express the conviction that the prophets and apostles (specifically David, Isaiah, Paul, and Peter) all spoke and wrote from the same Holy Spirit.[5]

When we come to Bede's commentary on the catholic epistles, we notice an interesting phenomenon: these epistles appear to be read in light of the book of Acts, whereas the reverse is not the case. That is, Acts seems to provide the historical and canonical foundation for the reading of these epistles. The catholic epistle collection was the last part of the New Testament to receive solid recognition throughout the Church as canonical. Bede's commentaries on Acts and these epistles provide the canon critic with an opportunity to see how an early interpreter of Scripture understood the relationship between Acts and the catholic epistles.

The reader gets the impression from his commentaries on the catholic epistles that Acts lies at the center of Bede's New Testament. For example, commenting on James 1:1 where the author addresses the twelve tribes "which are in the dispersion," Bede informs the reader that Acts describes the persecution that broke out in Jerusalem after Stephen was martyred, a persecution that caused all but the apostles to be dispersed throughout Judea and Samaria. According to Bede, the letter of James was addressed to these who "suffered persecution for righteousness sake." Here, Acts 8:1 provides the historical framework for Bede's reading of James. However, in his commentary on Acts 8:1, there is no reference to James. This function of Acts is further demonstrated by Bede's handling of James 3:1 ("do not a number of you, my brothers, become teachers, knowing that you are taking on a greater judgment"). Bede claims that certain teachers, coming down from Judea to Antioch, were teaching the necessity of circumcision according to the Mosaic Law, and that James was the one who had removed them and "teachers of their kind" from the responsibility of preaching the word so as not to hinder those who were preaching the truth. Here, Acts 15 provides the historical context for reading the warnings to teachers in James 3. Again, in his commentary on Acts 15, there is no reference to the epistle of James.[6]

---

[5] Bede does make a similar argument in his comments on 1 Peter 1:11-12 without, however, stating specifically that the argument "should have this place" in 1 Peter as he does in Acts. This Petrine text claims that the "Spirit of Christ" prophesied in the Old Testament prophets and that those who preached the gospel did so by the "Holy Spirit." Apparently, the argument which developed historically in conjunction with the text of Acts came to mind when Bede commented on the text of 1 Peter 1.

[6] Bede's commentary on the catholic epistles has a substantial number of references to Acts, mostly in the sections on James and 1 Peter. By contrast, there are very

In his commentary on 1 Peter, Bede identifies the recipients of the letter ("elect newcomers of the dispersion") with those present on the day of Pentecost when the Spirit was given. He informs the reader that there were certain from among the "newcomers" at Pentecost who, after the apostles had received the Spirit, believed in Christ through the apostolic preaching. He goes on to note, "but what is added, *of the dispersion,* means that they were dispersed from Jerusalem in the persecution that followed the death of Stephen . . . as we read in the Acts of the Apostles." So here again, the letter of Peter is read with Acts as a historical and canonical backdrop. Even Peter himself is characterized according to Acts. Commenting on 1 Peter 5:1 (where the author states that he is a "witness of the sufferings of Christ"), Bede claims that this means Peter stood near while Christ was suffering "or at least . . . he himself also suffered prison, chains, and scourging for the name of Christ, as we read in the Acts of the Apostles."[7]

Second Peter is also connected to Acts, albeit indirectly. In commenting on 2 Peter 1:1, Bede writes, "it has been written in what follows of this letter, *Look, dearly beloved, I am writing this second letter to you.* Hence it is clear that he wrote this letter . . . to the elect newcomers of the dispersion." Here the recipients of the letter are identified as those who received the first letter—recipients identified there with Acts.

Bede's commentary on the Johannine epistles contains few references to Acts. It is interesting to note, however, that one of those is probably a reference to Pentecost. In 1 John 3:24 the author states, "by this we know that he abides in us, by the Spirit that he has given us." Here Bede notes that in the earliest days of the Church the Spirit caused believers to speak in tongues that they had never studied. But now, he argues, the Church does not need external signs; rather, faith and love demonstrate the presence of the Spirit within the Christian. Why Bede needs to clarify this issue for his readers is unclear; it is not discussed in his commentary on Acts 2. It may simply be that Acts 2 comes into the

---

few references to the catholic epistles in his commentary on Acts. The reader gets the impression that for Bede, the epistles presuppose Acts while the reverse is not the case. Also, in his commentary on the epistles he consistently refers to Acts by its title, not its author, as if it transcends any one particular individual; whereas he regularly refers to other biblical books by their authors. There are a few instances in the commentary on Acts where he refers to Luke (i.e., "Luke shows/seems") but even here this is rare.

   [7] Bede also uses the Gospels to help characterize Peter and John in their epistles, something he cannot do for James the brother of Jesus.

commentary on 1 John 3 because of its great influence on Bede's pneumatology.[8]

Bede's commentary on Jude contains no explicit reference to Acts. However, he does claim that Jude is actually the apostle "whom Matthew and Mark in their Gospels call Thaddaeus." So Jude is explicitly associated with the Twelve, thus "tightening" the apostolic authorship of the New Testament canon, possibly under the influence of Acts with its establishment of the Twelve as the Church's foundational authorities.[9]

One more phenomenon relevant to the unifying function of Acts seen throughout Bede's commentaries needs to be considered. Harnack's proposal that Acts unifies the Gospels and Pauline epistles has been criticized for "confusing" the New Testament documents with the preaching of the apostles in Acts.[10] We have already noted the artificiality of this distinction from the patristic perspective.[11] Nowhere is this artificiality more clearly reinforced than in Bede's commentaries. He repeatedly makes the connection between the preaching of the apostles and the New Testament documents. In his commentary on James 1:1, Bede says of James, "he took care both to teach those present from among the circumcised by speaking to them and also to encourage, instruct, rebuke and correct the absent by letter." The Old Testament prophets "passed on the hidden heavenly mysteries which they had comprehended in secret to the people of God simply either by speaking or writing" (*Comm. on 2 Peter*, 133). Bede even notes that the teachers of the Church in his own day used both oral and written media to communicate the meaning of Scripture. He urges his readers to "seek first the simple basic elements of faith from . . . the Church, that is, from the teachers of the Old and New Testaments, who have either written or also preach to you orally the divine words . . ." (*Comm. on 1 Peter*, 80). For Bede, who depended heavily on the Church Fathers, Acts functioned as the unifier of the biblical canon, primarily by its pneumatology. This is seen partially by the comments which he makes in his

---

[8] For an excellent appraisal of the phenomenon of tongues-speaking, both ancient and modern, see Luke Timothy Johnson, "Glossolalia and the Embarrassments of Experience," *The Princeton Seminary Bulletin* 18/2 (1997) 113–34.

[9] Bede makes a similar claim for James the brother of Jesus, whom he claims is actually James the son of Alpheus, one of the Twelve. His discussion of this is found in his commentary on Acts 1:13.

[10] See, for example, the work of Kuck mentioned above.

[11] The Church Fathers appear to make no substantive distinction between the authority of the oral form and that of the written form. The key issue for them is the apostolic origin of the content.

commentary on Acts and partially from the way that Acts seems to function as a central reference point for his commentary on the catholic epistles.

But for Bede, Acts does not merely unite the canon. As with regard to his predecessors we must ask, *to what* does Acts unite the canon as a collection of witnesses for him? Throughout Bede's commentary on Acts, the text is read as a witness to a highly developed catholic trinitarian theology and to the hermeneutical authority of those who hold that theology. Furthermore, it is read as a witness against those who fail to conform to this ecclesiastical and theological paradigm. Thus, the patristic trend is continued and developed even further: Acts functions to unite the canonical voices as witnesses to the highly developed catholic system of thought of the late seventh and early eighth centuries and to thoroughly support the ecclesiastical authorities.

The appropriation of Acts as legitimation for episcopal hermeneutical authority is seen throughout Bede's commentary on Acts.[12] In fact, the commentary itself is written for and addressed to Bishop Acca, whom Bede describes in the preface as "his beatitude, most blessed in Christ, Lord Bishop Acca." Bede informs Acca that the very purpose of the canonical writings is to give confidence and authority to "subsequent teachers" (i.e., postapostolic authorities) in the Church. He ends the preface by wishing God's blessing on Acca so that he might guide and intercede for the Church. This episcopal acknowledgement on the part of Bede clearly sets the tone for the commentary.

In Acts 1:5 we read of Christ's prediction concerning the baptism of the Holy Spirit. This provides Bede with the opportunity to affirm the validity of catholic baptismal authority. He argues that the apostles and "their followers, who still baptize in the church to this day," possess the "interior power of the Holy Spirit" so that when the name of Christ is invoked the human administration of water purifies the recipients of baptism. The baptism of John, he argues, was unable to do this. Immediately in his commentary he has identified the ministry of the Spirit with the episcopacy. As the reader continues through the commentary, the appropriation of Luke's pneumatology for the simultaneous support of the unity of the canon and the hermeneutical authority of the catholic Church is evident.

Bede continues to appropriate the first chapter of Acts by claiming that Peter restored the number of apostles to twelve (by replacing Judas with Matthias) so that they might "certify the perfection of the work" that they were doing. This work is described as the preaching of "the

---

[12] As will be seen in the following analysis, this use of Acts is especially clear in the Acts 18–20 narrative, but is in no way limited to it.

faith of the holy Trinity" to the entire world. The patristic rule of faith has, by Bede's time, become a highly developed trinitarianism. But there is no concept of the historical development of theology in Bede's commentary. Bede does manifest a historical consciousness in his description of particular individuals, events, and other historical phenomena. In fact, Olsen concludes that while Bede accepts the traditional monastic reading of the descriptions of the early Church in Acts 2 and 4, he "broke new ground" in his tendency to see the primitive Church as having passed through stages of development.[13] With regard to the religious practices of the early Gentile Christians vis-à-vis their own pagan customs and the Mosaic Law, Olsen concludes that "Bede was alive to the process of organic development, and he assumed that the Gentiles had to go through a period of growth in Christianity and separation from their old manner of life."[14] But I would argue that Bede's use of the text of Acts to undergird the theology of the Church is itself rather ahistorical. He reads the highly developed version of the Trinity of his own day into the text of Acts and uses that interpretation to exclude interpretations of Christ and Scripture which do not conform to this understanding. For example, already in chapter one he finds occasion to condemn Arianism. Just as Judas died through the loss of his bodily organs (1:18), so "the heresiarch Arius" was condemned to a similar death. Bede argues that both Judas and Arius died a similar death because the former endeavored to destroy Christ's humanity while the latter endeavored to destroy Christ's divinity. Acts 1:18 becomes a sort of paradigm for heretics and their fate.

When we come to Peter's pentecostal sermon, we notice that in Bede's estimation Peter is preaching a post-Nicene Trinity and a post-Chalcedonian Christ. The Spirit descended at the third hour (2:15) "in order to proclaim to the world the glory of the indivisible Trinity." That Christ both received and poured out the Spirit (2:33) is evidence for Bede that "both natures of Christ are manifested," for he received the Spirit as a man and poured forth the Spirit as God. Peter's final injunction to repent and be baptized is significant for Bede for its supposed confirmation of catholic practice. Repentance is mentioned first, he notes, so that before being washed with water, they would first be washed with sorrow "in accordance with the church's practice," as if Peter was obligated by later ecclesiastical tradition. The three thousand who were baptized that day participated in the catholic Church's first

[13] Glenn Olsen, "Bede as Historian: The Evidence from His Observations on the Life of the First Christian Community at Jerusalem," *Journal of Ecclesiastical History* 33/4 (October 1982) 519.

[14] Ibid., 524.

baptism, according to Bede, and these were providentially gathered together "for the profession of the Holy Trinity."

As the commentary continues with Acts 3, a trend is begun which appears periodically throughout the work: the catholic authorities are identified with the apostles in a variety of ways. In 3:1, Peter and John heal a lame man at the Temple. They do this, according to Bede, because "the teachers of the church" preach first to Israel and then to the Gentiles. There is a subtle identification of the Church's "teachers" with the apostles here.[15] At the end of his Temple sermon (3:25-26), Peter asserts that God raised up His Son, the seed of Abraham. Bede argues that this is evidence of the two natures of the one Christ. Thus, it ought not be said that there is one son of man and one son of God. This, he argues, is "the trap of heresy in which the mad Manes and Nestorius were misled." Acts is here appropriated against the Manicheans and Nestorians and for the catholics.

Other noncatholic groups are condemned through Bede's use of Acts as well. The personification of the Holy Spirit in Acts 5:3 (Ananias' lying to the Spirit) is used as evidence for the deity and personality of the Spirit. For Bede, this text makes it clear that the Holy Spirit is God and that "the error of Macedonius had been condemned before he was born." Thus, the Macedonians are excluded and condemned by Bede's use of Acts.[16] But, on the other hand, the apostle Peter is a type of the catholic Church for Bede, and just as his shadow cured physical illness (5:15), so too the shadow of the Church spiritually renews those who partake of her sacraments.

This use of Acts to support the catholic ecclesiastical authority continues in Bede's comments on Acts 6:3 where the seven deacons are chosen. These officers, who rank above the laity, are chosen by the apostles "or the successors of the apostles throughout all of the churches." When we come to his comments on chapter 8, however, we notice an interesting phenomenon: there is not only a catholic succession for Bede, there is a heretical one as well. In Acts 8 we find the story of Simon the sorcerer who "believes" and is baptized under the ministry of the deacon Philip, and who then offers money to Peter for the power to confer the Spirit by the laying on of hands. Bede claims that Simon pretended to believe so that he could receive baptism and learn to perform Christian miracles. He then asserts that Simon's followers

---

[15] At other times in the commentary the connection is more explicit, as will be seen below.

[16] The Macedonians were a fourth-century sect that denied the divinity of the Holy Spirit. See the comments of L. T. Martin in Bede's *Commentary on Acts*, p. 62, n. 1.

were also taught to do this—to enter the church by deception and "to steal baptism." This "heretical" succession is immediately set in contrast with the apostolic succession and the authority which accompanies it. Bede argues that the Philip of Acts 8 must have been a deacon and not an apostle, otherwise he could have conferred the Spirit on others himself. But Peter and John had to come to Samaria for this purpose (8:14), for "this is reserved only to those of pontifical rank." After describing the catholic baptismal practices, Bede asserts, "This is reserved to the bishops alone when they transmit the Spirit, the Paraclete, to those who are baptized." The Spirit—the one who for Bede unites the canonical authorities according to the book of Acts—is transmitted to the baptized by the episcopal succession in the catholic Church. The text of Acts is being used to link the bishops with a united biblical canon, thus reinforcing the structure of authority promoted by the Fathers of the Church—a structure that includes both text and "true" interpretation of text.

Bede regularly employs allegorical interpretation to reinforce the legitimacy of the catholic hierarchy from the book of Acts. This allegorical interpretation is related to Bede's use of language in general, a use that frequently employs word association. That is, Bede seems to have associated the meaning and/or form of particular words with those of other words so that for him the primary word actually implied or suggested the second word.[17] For example, in commenting on Acts 8:27 (the story of the Ethiopian eunuch) Bede argues that the eunuch is called a *vir* (man) because although not physically sound, he possessed mental *virtute* (virtue).[18] Martin argues that Bede's understanding of language contains a richness provided by the "ambiguity of natural human language and metaphor" even while it forfeits a measure of precision.[19] This philosophy of language enables Bede to argue that the basket in which Paul escapes over the wall in Damascus (9:25) represents the Church which "even today" preserves "this sort of escape" from spiritual foes. The "great linen sheet" upon which Peter saw all sorts of unclean foods in a vision (10:11) "signifies the church" according to Bede, because the moth cannot corrupt it. Therefore, whoever wants to partake of "the mystery of the catholic church" must root out all corruption from the soul. The moth represents the "heretic [who] wishes to corrupt the Lord's robe." The four corners of the sheet represent

---

[17] Lawrence T. Martin, "Bede's Structural Use of Wordplay as a Way to Teach," *From Cloister to Classroom: Monastic and Scholastic Approaches to Truth,* ed. E. Elder (Kalamazoo, Mich.: Cistercian Publications, 1986) 27–46.

[18] Ibid., 35.

[19] Ibid., 45.

the four regions of the world to which the catholic Church extends. The threefold lowering of the sheet (10:12, 16) represents the unclean nations being cleansed "by the mystery of the holy Trinity in baptism." When the Church "kills and eats" (10:13) it devours that which is corrupt. But those who are "taken in by heretics" are devoured by death even while they live. Even Christ himself represents the Church at his baptism. Just as the Spirit descended upon him there (10:38), so the Spirit descends on the Church when it baptizes.

When we come to Bede's commentary on the Acts 18–20 narrative, the appropriation of the text to support the teaching authority of the Church is blatant. In 19:5 those who had only received John's baptism were baptized in the name of Jesus. This is not only evidence for Bede that John's baptism was insufficient, it also indicates for him the need to rebaptize those who were baptized in his own day by someone other than one who had participated in the episcopal succession. He argues that those who were baptized "apart from the succession" are in the same category as the followers of John; they stand in need of "Christ's baptism." He continues this line of argument in his comments on 19:7 where the text declares that twelve men were baptized in Ephesus. The number twelve is "the apostolic number" according to Bede. The Spirit fell on the 120 (which he notes is twelve multiplied by ten) in Jerusalem, the Jewish city, and on the twelve in Ephesus, the Greek city, to demonstrate that whether one is a Jew or a Gentile, the Spirit fills "only those who share in the unity of the catholic and apostolic church." To strengthen his case even more, he argues that the seven sons of Sceva (19:14f.) represent all those who oppose the catholic Church. The number seven, he claims, represents the gifts of the Holy Spirit, gifts falsely claimed by Sceva's sons. "Sceva," he says, means "a yelping little fox." This shrewd and deceitful animal represents "the Jews, gentiles, and heretics, who are always plotting against the church of God" (19:14). The bishops, whom he here calls "the guardians of the church," must "catch the tiny foxes" before they wreck the vineyard, as the Song of Solomon describes (2:15).

These guardians are especially obligated to interpret Scripture properly according to Bede. In Acts 20:7-12 Luke records the story of Eutychus, the young lad who fell out of the window during Paul's lengthy midnight sermon. Bede interprets the text allegorically to argue that the upper room represents the spiritual gifts of the Church, the night represents "the obscurity of scriptures," and the lamps represent "the explanation of the more enigmatic sayings." This passage warns the ecclesiastical teachers that they must shed light on these enigmas for the sake of weak listeners "just as the apostle did." And finally, in commenting on Paul's exhortations to the Ephesian bishops (the last pericope in the Acts 18–20 narrative), Bede argues that Paul's reference to his three years of teaching (20:31) is to be understood as his threefold interpretation of Scripture: the historical, moral, and typological senses of the text. Thus, in Bede's commentary on Acts 18–20, the appropriation of the text in support of the teaching authority of the catholic hierarchy is clearly seen. The hermeneutics of the Church are the hermeneutics of Paul, and all noncatholic interpretations of Scripture and sacramental activities are fraudulent.

The rest of Bede's commentary on Acts reinforces all of these things. A rather fully developed trinitarian theology is repeatedly upheld by means of the text, the teaching authority of the episcopal succession is reinforced, and all other perspectives are excluded. Both literal and allegorical methods of interpretation are used to strengthen his arguments for this ecclesiastical structure.

Thus, the Venerable Bede has found value in the text of Acts to do two things simultaneously. First, he argues that the canonical documents are unified in their witness to catholic dogma. Second, he uses the text—especially but not exclusively the Acts 18–20 narrative—to undergird the hermeneutical authority of the catholic Church. For Bede, Acts demonstrates the united witness of Scripture to the trinitarian theology of the Church, a theology determined by those participating in the apostolic succession. He has taken what was given to him by the fathers and has developed it even further. He provides a synthesis and recapitulation of the patristic use of Acts in a more explicit and developed form. A structure (canon and interpretive office) which was originally designed to combat Gnosticism in its various forms—including the Marcionite version—has become a permanent element in catholic Christianity. Acts, being relevant to both elements of this structure, provides Bede with a sort of container into which any "heresy" can be placed and condemned. And, as noted above, Bede influenced many who came after him in the Church—something which makes his use of Acts even more significant.

What Irenaeus and Tertullian created, Cyril incorporated and John Chrysostom developed further. And to that which his predecessors created, incorporated, and developed, Bede gave full expression. During the late second and early third centuries, the function of Acts as a unifier of the developing canon was clearly established through the use of that text in the polemical debates of the time, and the episcopal argument was primarily based on oral tradition, the text of Acts serving as a secondary reinforcement. But as ecclesiastical literary works multiplied, the text of Acts was increasingly used for both elements of the argument. By the late patristic and early medieval periods, Acts could be used by the catholic authorities to appropriate the entire canon for their own purposes and to exclude all opposing perspectives. The structure of the catholic canon from the fourth century on can be illustrated by the following graph:

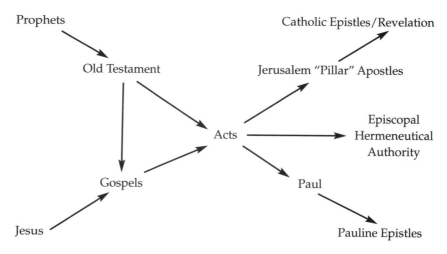

Illustration 2: The Structure of the Catholic Canon

Acts provided the organizing centerpiece for the primary catholic collection of religiously authoritative texts through its unification of the canonical and ecclesiastical authorities (the prophets, Jesus, Jerusalem apostles, Paul, and "bishops") by means of the Spirit.[20] It gave the catholic hierarchy a basis for claiming the biblical documents as their own vis-à-vis all other interpretations of the Christian traditions. The authority of Acts can be described in terms of the ecclesiastical definition given to canon in the Introduction above. This functional definition of canon is given as "the boundaries of orthodoxy and the textual basis for the authority of community leaders."[21] Although the association of its author Luke with an apostle gave the document *a priori* authority, it was the internal characteristics of the document which gave it great value for the Church and which pushed it into the very center of the canon. It aided the developing catholic hierarchy in its attempt to define the boundaries of orthodoxy and seemed to give them a basis for promoting their own hermeneutical authority.

[20] The phrase "organizing centerpiece" as a description of my understanding of the function of Acts in the patristic canon was first suggested to me by Khalid Blankinship of Temple University.

[21] See Introduction, page 13.

Chapter 4

A Comparative Analysis
of the Apocryphal Acts

The value of Acts for catholic Christianity in the structuring of both canon and community becomes even clearer when it is compared to the various noncanonical Acts. Throughout the second and third centuries, various Acts of particular apostles were composed, works that honored the legendary deeds of these early Christian heroes. The five primary apocryphal Acts are the Acts of Peter, Paul, John, Andrew, and Thomas.[1]

In this chapter I am not interested in judging the orthodoxy of these writings, their historical reliability, their possible dependence on earlier sources (including canonical Acts), or the quality of their literary form.[2] I simply want to ask the following question: Do these Acts possess the characteristics that canonical Acts does, characteristics that enabled the Fathers to argue for a unified canonical witness to catholic trinitarianism?

There is a danger inherent in such a comparison, however. Richard Pervo describes the traditional scholarly comparison of Acts and apocryphal Acts as follows:

> As a widely-held notion would have it: once upon a time there were any number of Gospels and Acts engaged in competition for biblical status. . . . This popular belief, that Christian apocrypha simply imitated their canonical antecedents with the goal of inclusion within the Bible, is incorrect.[3]

[1] Richard I. Pervo, "Early Christian Fiction," *Greek Fiction: The Greek Novel in Context*, ed. J. R. Morgan and R. Stoneman (New York: Routledge, 1994) 242.

[2] Except, of course, as these have direct bearing on the issue of ecclesiastical authority.

[3] Pervo, "Early Christian Fiction," 241.

In the analysis which follows, I am not assuming that the authors of the apocryphal Acts competed for anything like canonical status. Pervo has argued that the ancient Christian Acts (including canonical Acts) are essentially novels which both instruct and entertain.[4] To the extent that he is correct, one need not assume a "canonical" goal for any of the Acts. Nevertheless, the Lukan Acts was in fact the only Acts canonized by the Church; therefore, scholars of early Christianity ought to continue to investigate the reasons for this decision.

One could argue that the dates of composition of the apocryphal Acts were sufficient reason for their noncanonical status; Pervo assigns all of the major apocryphal Acts to the period of ca. 150–250 C.E.[5] It seems fairly clear from early Christian sources that writings known (or believed) to have been written at such a late date were excluded in spite of their positive qualities. But the criterion of date of composition is insufficient in determining the status of a document vis-à-vis the canon, as the rejection of certain early documents (like 1 *Clement*) demonstrates.

Nor is it possible to dismiss the apocryphal Acts completely as a group based on theological content, in spite of the later popularity of the five major Acts among the Manichaeans.[6] This is the case for two reasons. First, these Acts are not theologically homogeneous. One detects both catholic and Gnostic ideas within the same text and varying degrees of both from text to text. This should not be surprising, given the lack of absolute distinction between "orthodox" and "heretical" groups before the fourth century. In fact, Ehrman points to these Acts as some of the best indicators of pre-Nicene theological imprecision. He is correct in his observation that these Acts represent theological views that "at times appear orthodox and at times heretical."[7] Second, these texts

---

[4] Ibid., 239–44.

[5] Ibid., 242.

[6] See J. K. Elliott, *The Apocryphal New Testament* (Oxford: Clarendon Press, 1993) 229.

[7] Bart D. Ehrman, *The Orthodox Corruption of Scripture* (New York: Oxford University Press, 1993) 10–11. For Ehrman's nuanced use of the terms "orthodox" and "heretical" see Introduction, note 27, above. Although there are Gnostic elements in the various Acts, it would be inaccurate to categorize all of them as Gnostic texts per se, for the Gnostic elements are not uniform throughout each text. For example, the Acts of Peter demonstrates a more identifiable Gnosticism in the final Martyrdom section than in the sections that precede it. A part of the problem of identifying the theological nature of these texts lies in the largely unknown history of their redaction, including the combination of diverse sources that enjoyed previous and even subsequent independent existence. This redaction has produced texts that are not necessarily theologically consistent throughout.

and the various traditions contained within them did not receive uniform response from the Church Fathers.[8] For example, although the Acts of Paul was rejected by Tertullian as the work of a well-meaning but misguided Asian presbyter (*On Baptism* 17), it is included in the list of canonical writings inserted into the sixth-century codex Claromontanus (D), a Greek and Latin manuscript of the epistles of Paul. This list may have been drawn up as early as 300 C.E.[9] In fact, Metzger goes so far as to identify these Acts as "books of temporary and local canonicity."[10] The point here is that these writings and particular traditions contained within them were variously accepted and rejected during the history of the early Church so that a simple rejection of them on the basis of the criterion of "orthodoxy" is difficult if not impossible.[11]

Whatever else may have contributed to the noncanonical status of these works, here I will confine my comparative analysis to the issue of ecclesiastical authority as described above; that is, the ability of canonical Acts: (1) to demonstrate the unity of the Israelite prophets, Jesus of Nazareth, the Jerusalem apostles, Paul, and the canonical writings associated with them, by means of the Holy Spirit, and (2) to provide a basis for postapostolic hermeneutical authority, also through its pneumatology. Do the apocryphal Acts possess the same qualities? In what follows I examine the apocryphal Acts of the three primary apostles of the New Testament: Peter, John, and Paul.[12]

The Acts of Peter

The apocryphal Acts of Peter lacks the kind of unifying structure found in the book of Acts, though a few of these unifying elements can be found scattered throughout the work. There are a handful of references that affirm the unity of Peter and Paul and there are no hints at any strife between them. Paul apparently speaks well of Peter, for

---

[8] Cf. Elliott, *Apocryphal NT*, 350.

[9] Bruce M. Metzger, *The Canon of the New Testament: Its Origin, Development, and Significance* (Oxford: Oxford University Press, 1987) 310. Next to the Acts of Paul and several other noncanonical works in this list is a scribal mark, one that Metzger theorizes may indicate a lesser status (230).

[10] Ibid., 165.

[11] A good example of a tradition from an apocryphal Acts that became well accepted in the Church is the story of Peter's crucifixion upside-down recorded in the Acts of Peter 37. This is not to say that the Acts of Peter was the only or even the primary source of the story; but minimally it illustrates the overlap that existed between "apocryphal" and "orthodox" traditions.

[12] Unless otherwise noted, all quotations from the apocryphal Acts are taken from Elliott, *Apocryphal NT*.

Ariston is quoted as saying, "Since Paul has gone to Spain . . . I have fled from Rome hoping for the arrival of Peter. For Paul had spoken of him, and I saw many things in a vision" (6). Similarly, Marcellus tells Peter that he has learned from his "fellow-apostle Paul" (10). But beyond this, there is no linking of these two apostles with anyone else.

The references to the prophets of ancient Israel in the Acts of Peter are also quite rare, and when they are quoted there is confusion as to which of the prophets spoke which particular oracle. For example, two passages from Isaiah 53 are quoted by Peter in the narrative but are assigned to two different anonymous prophets. Also, one of them is assigned two oracles not found in the Hebrew Bible (24).

Most significant is the scarcity of references in the Acts of Peter to the Holy Spirit. Paul and Peter are said to be filled with the Holy Spirit only once each. Peter baptizes Theon in the name of the Father, Son, and Holy Spirit, but neither he nor any other convert is ever said to have received the Spirit. And the account of Peter's confrontation with Simon the magician in Judea, which plays a significant role in the narrative of the Acts of Peter, differs significantly from the account found in canonical Acts precisely on the subject of the Holy Spirit. In the Lukan Acts Peter's fury is aroused because of Simon's desire to purchase the ability to give the Holy Spirit. But in the apocryphal account, Peter rebukes and exiles Simon for using magic to commit larceny; there is no reference to the Spirit in the account. There are several references to "the spirit" in the final "Martyrdom" section, but the Gnostic character of this section of the Acts of Peter makes it difficult to know whether this is a reference to the Holy Spirit or to the realm of spirit (in general). Therefore, I conclude that the Acts of Peter would not have had the kind of unifying value for the catholic bishops that the Lukan Acts possesses.

Is there anything in the text of the Acts of Peter that could be appropriated by the catholic bishops to support their claims of apostolic succession? The answer is no. There is virtually nothing in the text to support this claim. In fact, the text seems to undermine this idea in a number of ways. First, there is the absence of any apostolic provision for postapostolic authority. There is nothing comparable to the narrative of Acts 18–20, where the Spirit conferred by Paul appoints bishops. There is one anomalous reference to a young man who will someday "serve as deacon and bishop" (27), but this is never explained or developed in the text and seems out of place. One can only speculate as to its meaning here. Second—and most significantly—there is in the text of the Acts of Peter an exaltation of the apostles Paul and (especially) Peter of such a nature that no one can take their place. In fact, as the story unfolds the believing communities virtually disintegrate whenever the apostles leave town. As the story begins, Paul is in Rome "confirming many in the faith" when he sees in a vision the Lord beckoning him to Spain. When the believers hear of Paul's intention to leave, they experience great lamentation and beg him not to desert them "like children without a mother" (1). As he is preparing to leave, the believers bring the elements to him so that he might offer them the Eucharist one last time. Paul responds with rebuke, warning them to repent of their sins. His hearers doubt whether God has forgiven them and they pray that God would bring Paul back to them safely because they perceive their own weakness (2).

This complete dependence on the apostle and the lack of any provision for postapostolic authority is continually reinforced throughout the story. After Paul's departure, Simon the sorcerer, whom Peter had confronted and expelled from Judea, arrives in Rome, causing great distress among the Christians. The narrator identifies the absence of Paul and his companions as the cause of this great alarm (4). Simon deceives all but a few of the Christians by his magic, causing these few to pray for Paul's speedy return or the arrival of someone else to deliver those "whom the devil by his wickedness had perverted" (4).

The answer to this prayer comes in the form of Peter's arrival in Rome. The heart of the story is Peter's extended confrontation of Simon. Both men perform miracles in a contest for the devotion of the people. In the end, Peter outperforms Simon and the believing community is restored. Here, only an apostle can take the place of an apostle; the idea of an apostolic successor is lacking.

In the final "Martyrdom" section of the Acts of Peter, Peter begins to leave Rome after hearing of a plot to end his life, when the Lord instructs him to return and suffer martyrdom there. Upon his return the believing community is still overwhelmed by its own spiritual weakness and they implore Peter to help them. Peter responds by assuring them that God is able to strengthen their faith, but there is no provision for overseers to be given to the community after his death.

The answer to the problem of the community's weakness is provided by the narrator through the mouth of Peter as he approaches the cross upon which he is to be crucified, and after he is placed on that cross. Peter delivers two sermons here, both of which promote the Gnostic method of attaining spiritual knowledge and transformation. Truth, he argues, is known and understood through direct spiritual perception within one's own soul. Peter urges his hearers to avoid all that is perceived by the senses and to withdraw from "outward" actions (37). They are to listen to that divine voice which is "heard through silence" and which "does not come through the organs of the body" (39). Interestingly, Peter also argues that this voice "is not written in books" (39).

What we have in the apocryphal Acts of Peter is an alternative to the catholic religious structure. In the Acts of Peter religious truth is known by an internal gnosis that transcends text and tradition. The apostle makes known this method of knowledge and salvation. It appears to be the *method* of gaining spiritual knowledge that is "canonized" by this text and those Gnostics who valued it.[13] It is not difficult to see why this text would not have served the interests of the catholics: both elements of their structure of authority (canonical text and ecclesiastical office) are undermined and an alternative system is proposed.

The Acts of John

As we approach the text of the apocryphal Acts of John, we again want to look for elements within the text that could be used by the developing catholic hierarchy to argue for a unified canon and the legitimacy of the episcopal office and hermeneutical claim—or elements that seem to undermine either or both of these ideas. With regard to the uniting of the canonical authorities by means of the Spirit, we find very little of this in the Acts of John. A few times John appeals to sayings of Jesus found in the Gospels, as when he prays, "For you have said yourself, O Christ, 'Ask and it shall be given you'" (22). There are also a few references to the other apostles, as when John affirms that Jesus "had chosen Peter and Andrew" (88) and when he tells the story of Jesus taking "[him] and James and Peter to the mountain" (90). However, these apostles are subsequently portrayed as somewhat inferior to John. While on the mountain, John approaches Jesus alone "because he [Jesus] loved me" and John receives special revelation from Christ (90). Having realized what happened, Peter and James become angry with John whereupon he advises them to receive knowledge directly from Christ as he had (91).

With regard to the Old Testament prophets, there is a similar ambiguity. There are some pericopes found in certain Latin manuscripts that may or may not be a part of the original Acts of John.[14] In them there are a few positive references to the Old Testament. The first two are contained in the retelling of the story of the rich man and Lazarus from Luke 16:19-31 where Abraham tells the rich man that the latter's five brothers ought to heed the warnings of "Moses and the prophets" (VI). In the third reference the author affirms that the Holy Spirit spoke "by the prophet" whereupon he quotes from a Psalm (VI). And finally, God

---

[13] These Acts were valued by the Manichaeans and other anonymous "heretics." See the comments of Elliott, *Apocryphal NT*, 303, 390.

[14] See the textual-critical discussion in Elliott, *Apocryphal NT*, 304–06.

is said to have spoken concerning the salvation of sinners in Ezekiel 33:11 (VII). Militating against the inclusion of these pericopes in the original Acts of John, however, is one of the two clear references to the Old Testament in the undisputed portion of the text. In the first, John refers to the "lawless Jews, who received their law from a lawless serpent" (94). This betrays a rather obvious rejection of the Old Testament by the anonymous author(s) of the Acts of John. The second reference is positive but qualified. Here John affirms that God had revealed himself "through the Law and the prophets," but he also claims that God had made himself known "through all nature, even among the animals" (112). These conflicting references to the Old Testament make it difficult to determine the author's (or authors') attitude toward the Old Testament canon.

Is there any provision in this text for an apostolic succession or teaching office? Throughout the Acts of John, John himself is the incomparable hero, performing great miracles (including many resurrections from the dead) and persuading many. Those who believe his message are portrayed as deeply dependent upon him for spiritual sustenance. In Ephesus, the people touch him and cry out, "Help us John, help us who die in vain!" (44). Again they plead, "[Give] us, we beseech you, help without hindrance . . . [receive] us who are desperate!" (44). John promises not to leave Ephesus until he has weaned them like children and set them "upon a firm rock" (45).

But soon the people of Smyrna hear of John and send messengers to Ephesus who implore him to come there and to the surrounding cities that they might come to know his God and hope in him (55). John comes to Smyrna, performs a great miracle, and instructs them in the faith. After some time passes he informs the Smyrnans that he must make a pastoral visit to the Ephesians "so that they may not become slack" because of his absence (58). Upon hearing this, the Smyrnans become "distressed" and "sad that they should be separated from him" (58). John's advice is telling. There is no provision for postapostolic leadership. He simply tells them that though he must leave, Christ is always with them. Communion with Christ will bring the blessing they seek (58). Nevertheless, when John leaves to return to Ephesus, he leaves the believers "sorrowing and weeping" (59). Many, in fact, accompany him, refusing to be separated from him (59).

Throughout the story the reader is given the impression that no one can take the place of John. His power and knowledge are unmatched by anyone. Learning the art of personal communion with Christ is the only solution offered to the problem of John's departure. In fact, as John is preparing for death, he claims that God had appeared to him when he was young and had called him to apostleship by exclaiming, "I am in need of you, John" (113). So from this perspective, even God needs the apostle John!

The two key characteristics of the Lukan Acts of the Apostles that gave it value in the eyes of the Church Fathers are virtually absent from the Acts of John. There is very little linking of John's preaching or writings with other canonical authorities, and that which is present is inconsistent.[15] Furthermore, there is no provision for ecclesiastical leadership. This is underscored by the scarcity of references to the Spirit in the Acts of John. Only occasionally is John (or any other canonical authority) said to be moved by the Spirit in his preaching or performance of miracles, and only once is the Spirit associated with the Church in a meaningful way.[16] I conclude that there is no solid basis in the text for claiming either a united canon or episcopal hermeneutical authority.

The Acts of Paul

The apocryphal Acts of Paul is in some ways difficult to analyze due to its structure. It includes three main sections and some fragmentary additional ones. The three main sections are "The Acts of Paul and Thecla," "The Corinthian Correspondence," and "The Martyrdom of

[15] There is, however, a relevant reference to John's two modes of communication that underscores my insistence, noted throughout this project, that in the eyes of the early Christians there was no substantial difference between the oral and written modes of "apostolic" teaching as far as the issue of religious *authority* was concerned. During one sermon, John exclaims that he will communicate to his hearers those things that he believes they are capable of understanding and in a way that they can grasp. This will be somewhat difficult for him because in reality spiritual truth is ineffable. He declares, "I, indeed, am able neither to set forth to you nor to write the things which I saw and heard" (88). The point here is that there is an assumption on the part of the author(s) that whether John speaks or writes, his apostolic authority stands behind the declaration, inadequate though it may be. This phenomenon is seen throughout early Christian literature, one that explains the ease with which the fathers could use Acts to unite the writings of the New Testament—and not just the speeches of the apostles—with those of the Old Testament prophets. There may have been a difference in the way oral and written communication were understood to have *affected* one's audience in early Christianity, as when Paul describes preaching as the demonstration of the Spirit's power (1 Cor 2:4), but it appears that relatively equal authority lay behind the two modes of communication.

[16] Here the Spirit is described as the "illuminator and sanctifier of the whole Church." This reference is found in one of the questionable pericopes (V). Beyond this, there are a few references to the Trinity in one form or another throughout the text.

Paul," all three of which appear to have had an independent existence prior to and even after their grouping under the heading "The Acts of Paul."[17]

Throughout most of the Acts of Paul, the characteristics of canonical Acts which are at issue in this project are absent. In the Acts of Paul and Thecla, the Holy Spirit is never mentioned.[18] The Father and the Son are repeatedly addressed and referred to, but neither Paul nor Thecla nor anyone else is ever filled with the Spirit nor do they perform miracles by the Spirit. The reader almost gets the impression that Paul himself plays the role of the Spirit in this work. For example, after Thecla has been condemned to be burned, she looks for Paul "as a lamb in the wilderness looks around for the shepherd" (21). Having looked throughout the crowd, the author of our text tells us that "she saw the Lord sitting in the likeness of Paul and said, 'As if I were unable to endure, Paul has come to look after me.' And she gazed upon him with great earnestness, but he went up into heaven" (par. 21). So the Lord strengthens Thecla through the image of Paul and not through the Holy Spirit. Other episodes in which we might expect a reference to the Spirit similarly lack any such reference. Such is the case, for example, during the episode of Thecla's baptism. We are told that the event was accompanied by lightning and a cloud of fire, but the Holy Spirit is not mentioned. Furthermore, there is no quoting of the prophets of Israel nor any connection with them nor with any other apostles by means of the Holy Spirit.

Some of these elements are, however, present in the latter portions of the Acts of Paul, beginning with Paul's apocryphal letter to the Corinthians and ending with his martyrdom. The authors of these sections (and the short narrative link between them) appear to have been much more acquainted with the canonical Acts, for they include several of the kinds of references to the Holy Spirit, the ancient prophets, and the other apostles which we find in the Lukan Acts. For example, in the apocryphal epistle Paul claims that he received the gospel tradition from the apostles before him "who were always with Jesus Christ," and he affirms the role of the Holy Spirit in the virginal conception of Jesus and in the ministry of the prophets of ancient Israel (5–10).

In the short narrative link which follows and in the subsequent martyrdom account, we encounter Spirit-terminology reminiscent of

---

[17] Elliott, *Apocryphal NT*, 350–57.

[18] The only exception is one apparently late manuscript which includes a final prayer by Thecla addressed to the Father, Son, and Holy Spirit, and a concluding remark by the redactor giving glory to the Father, Son, and Holy Spirit. See Elliott, *Apocryphal NT*, 372–74.

canonical Acts. Paul is said to be full of the Holy Spirit when he addresses the believing community and when he responds to Nero's inquiry. He also receives knowledge from the Spirit—knowledge he would not otherwise possess. Furthermore, the prophetess Myrta speaks of Paul's imminent departure to Rome by means of the Spirit. All of these references set the final sections of the Acts of Paul apart from the previous sections (including the Acts of Paul and Thecla) where this kind of Spirit-terminology is absent. Thus it would seem that the Acts of Paul had no unifying structure of its own, borrowing in a few sections from the canonical book of Acts. This conclusion is further supported by an episode in the martyrdom narrative in which a certain Patroclus, cupbearer of Nero, sat on a high window listening to Paul preach in Rome and fell from the window and died. Paul then raises him from the dead and sends him on his way. This is an obvious borrowing of the Eutychus episode in Acts 20.

Not only is there very little in the Acts of Paul which would have been of value to the catholics in their attempt to unify the canon, there is little that could have been appropriated to support the claims of apostolic episcopal succession. As I have noted above, (canonical) Acts 18–20 provided a reinforcement for the episcopal claim with its portrayal of Paul as dispenser of the Spirit and the (Ephesian) recipients as Spirit-appointed "bishops." There is nothing comparable to this in the Acts of Paul. The closest parallels are the healing ministry of Thecla and the brief references to the baptizing ministry of Titus and Luke—all three of whom were companions of Paul. But the idea of succession is missing as is the pneumatology of Acts 18–20. And in regard to Thecla's baptism, she administers it to herself—a phenomenon which the catholic Fathers apparently could not accept, given their insistence on episcopal (and male) baptismal authority. Thus I conclude that the Acts of Paul could not have functioned in the way canonical Acts could (and did) for the catholic bishops of the late second century and following.

Conclusion

The apocryphal Acts had widespread appeal among the laity in ancient Christianity. Metzger argues that the meager amount of space given to any particular apostle in canonical Acts encouraged the production of these various Acts, novels that replaced the obscenities of the Greco-Roman novels with "moralizing calculated to provide instruction in Christian piety."[19] Pervo argues that these writings reflect the interests not so much of marginal groups but of the more ordinary

---

[19] Metzger, *The Canon*, 174.

early Christian believers.[20] Included among these interests were: (1) power, including the power to remove the misfortunes of hunger, disease, and even death, and the power to resist oppressive rulers; and (2) the wish for excitement.[21] These needs were symbolically met through the legendary tales of the apostles. Pervo makes an interesting observation with regard to the resolution of theological dissension within the texts of the apocryphal Acts themselves. He argues that the popular nature of these writings is manifested by the fact that "heretics" and "heresies" are not refuted by argumentation; they are defeated by the demonstration of superior supernatural power.[22] For example, in the Acts of Peter, the heart of the drama involves the showdown between Peter and Simon. While Simon demonstrates amazing supernatural powers, Peter always "outdoes" him, and in the end Peter's miracles are more persuasive to the crowds than are those of Simon. Gallagher makes a convincing case that these Acts were not only instrumental in the conversions of substantial numbers of people to Christianity, but that they also reveal well-developed understandings of what conversion means.[23]

While these conclusions concerning the popular appeal of the apocryphal Acts are not without merit, in my judgment they fail to provide adequate explanation for the noncanonical status of these writings within catholic Christianity. The preceding analysis has demonstrated that the authors of these Acts not only avoided providing a basis in their texts for the catholic appropriation of all the canonical witnesses and for the legitimation of the catholic hierarchy, they created narratives that actually seemed to undermine these two elements in the catholic structure of authority (canon and interpretation of canon). This undermining occurred chiefly by two means. First, individual apostles are glorified in the texts, a glorification that sometimes seems to actually "confuse" the apostle with Christ himself—including the visionary appearances of the apostle both before and after his death.[24] This individual apostolic glorification stands in contrast to the presentation of the apostles as a unified, ecclesiologically foundational group of witnesses

[20] Pervo, "Early Christian Fiction," 242.

[21] Ibid., 242–43.

[22] Ibid., 249.

[23] Eugene V. Gallagher, "Conversion and Salvation in the Apocryphal Acts of the Apostles," *The Second Century: A Journal of Early Christian Studies* 8/1 (Spring 1991) 16. Gallagher argues that the many resurrection episodes (especially in the Acts of John and Peter) serve to illustrate the understanding of conversion as a rebirth resulting in eternal life.

[24] François Bovon, *New Testament Traditions and Apocryphal Narratives*, trans. Jane Haapiseva-Hunter (Allison Park: Pickwick Publications, 1995) 170.

in canonical Acts, and, as Bovon notes, these apocryphal conceptions of the apostolate always concentrate the power of God on the strength of the apostle, not on his weakness, contrary to the theology of the Pauline epistles (2 Cor 12:7-10).[25] Second, in keeping with the glorification of the apostles, there is no provision for an apostolic succession. The operative assumption appears to be the conviction that no one could measure up to or replace the apostle. The knowledge of truth comes not by the passing on of doctrine by means of the episcopacy, but through existential spiritual experience, if at all. Any provision for an apostolic succession would likely have lessened the esteem given to the apostle by the author and the readers of the Acts, and would have detracted from the excitement of the account.

Through the texts of the apocryphal Acts, individual believers could take solace in the power of the apostles without the encumbrances of the ecclesiastical hierarchy. Visions of and from Christ and the apostles were possible in this model, as exhibited throughout the texts of these Acts. Bovon argues that it was not solely the Montanists and their revelatory claims that the early catholic leadership had to resist, but also those enamored by the legends of the apostles and the "proliferation of visions and [the] doctrinal and ecclesial privileges which [these Gnostics] were claiming."[26]

The Lukan Acts provided for both the glorification of the apostles and the control of that glorification. Although not lacking in apostolic miracle, canonical Acts emphasizes the orderly spreading of the apostolic message which, according to Luke, was predicted by the prophets and fulfilled in Jesus, and it includes provision for postapostolic ecclesiastical leadership. These characteristics gave the Lukan Acts great value for the developing catholic hierarchy and precluded the canonization of other Acts.

---

[25] Bovon, *NT Traditions*, 170.
[26] Ibid.

Conclusion

Acts and Contemporary Issues

I conclude this study of the canonical function of Acts with some brief thoughts on the connection between the patristic use of Acts and contemporary issues of concern. These issues include the influence of theological presuppositions on the shape of the Bible, the Christian use of the Old Testament, the structure of ecclesiastical authority, unity and diversity within Christianity, and contemporary canon studies. These observations are intended to suggest further avenues for research.

Presuppositions

Fundamentally, Marcion rejected the writings of the Old Testament because he rejected the God of the Old Testament. He brought this presupposition to the table and it determined his concept of canon to a large extent. His semi-Gnostic dualistic world view led him to believe that the God proclaimed and revealed by Jesus was the only God who was worthy of worship and faith, and in his view it was Paul alone among the apostles who understood the message of Jesus. The Pauline antithesis between the Mosaic Law and Christ was evidence for Marcion that both could not be represented side by side in a sacred literary canon, the former representing the will of the demiurge and the latter revealing the highest God for the first time in history. In light of this, his "Gospel and Apostle" canon, containing a version of the Gospel of Luke (which was associated with Paul) and ten Pauline epistles makes sense. It was strictly a "Pauline" Christ that Marcion was interested in promoting and his canon reflected this.

The catholics, on the other hand, rejected the Creator-Redeemer bifurcation implicit in the Gnostic world view, arguing that the Creator-God was the same Being as the Redeemer-God. For them, the God who had created the world and had granted revelation through the prophets of ancient Israel was the same God whom Jesus had come to reveal and all the apostles had proclaimed. This too sheds light on their conception of what a sacred literary canon ought to look like. Since they believed that the same God had granted revelation through the prophets of ancient Israel, Jesus, the apostles associated with the Jerusalem church, and Paul, it is understandable that their canon should include the Old Testament, the Gospels, the catholic epistles and Apocalypse, and the Pauline epistles.[1] It is also not surprising that with such a diverse canon they would include an element that in some way would unite all of these into a coherent whole and give at least some textual support to their claims of hermeneutical authority. This was, of course, the canonical function of Acts, which portrays all of the canonical authorities working under the guidance of the same Holy Spirit to accomplish the will of God in the world, and which seems to sanction a form of apostolic succession by means of that Spirit.

This study has brought to light a fundamental principle of the formation of the biblical canon. The presuppositions of the catholic Christian community played a major role in both the theoretical and the actual shape of their canon and in the broad hermeneutical principles applied to those texts by the canonizing community. What the early Christians believed about the world and its relationship to the divine determined the broad confines within which various texts were recognized as religiously authoritative and were interpreted. Because the catholic Christians believed the Creator, and not another God, had sent Jesus with the message of redemption, they accepted the Scriptures which testified to the Creator and incorporated them into their sacred literary canon. The author of Acts shared this presupposition and his text supported the community in its decision to unite old and new texts into one collection. Greater insight into the Christian Scriptures—as well as the sacred texts of other religions—will be gained as scholars continue to identify and analyze the presuppositions of those who produced, valued, and preserved those texts.

The Christian Use of the Old Testament

The catholic Christian recognition of the Scriptures of ancient Israel as authoritative in the Church was supported by Luke and reinforced by the canonization of the text of Acts. This inclusion of the Old Testament has mandated the use of these texts by Christians in some way—

---

[1] My point is not that the precise make-up of the canon was inevitable, but simply that the final form of the canon makes sense in light of catholic presuppositions.

but how? To what extent has Christianity established clear guidelines for the use of the Old Testament? I would argue that the central hermeneutical principle here has been christology, but beyond this there has been disagreement over the use of the Old Testament in the faith and practice of the Church. That is, from the beginning Christians have read the former Scriptures from the perspective of the event of Christ, seeing various aspects of his person and work in a variety of Old Testament passages. For example, Matthew regularly cites biblical texts in his Gospel narrative, claiming that a particular event took place in the life of Jesus in order that the Scripture "might be fulfilled." When he quotes a passage like Zechariah 9:9 ("Lo, your king comes to you . . . riding on a donkey") and argues that it has been fulfilled *(plēroō)* in an act of Jesus (21:4-5), he is using a text that appears to be messianic in its original context. But Matthew also feels free to quote texts that do not appear to be either messianic or eschatological, and to claim "fulfillment" in Jesus. For example, in Psalm 78:2 we read of Asaph's determination to "open [his] mouth in a parable" and to "utter dark sayings from of old." Matthew claims that Jesus' use of parables "fulfills" this text, a text "spoken through the prophet" (13:34-35). In Matthew's reading, Asaph is a prophet who in some sense foreshadows or predicts the use of parables by the Messiah.

These kinds of christological readings of the Old Testament are found throughout the New Testament and the literature of the early Church and have continued to the present day within Christianity.[2] But beyond this basic shared conviction, Christians have disagreed over a number of issues related to the use of the Old Testament. One such issue is the debate over allegorical interpretation, a debate that surfaced in the early Church and has continued to manifest itself in a number of ways throughout the history of biblical interpretation.[3] Another

[2] For a good analysis of Matthew's use of Scripture, see Graham Stanton, "Matthew," *It Is Written: Scripture Citing Scripture,* ed. D. Carson and H. Williamson (New York: Cambridge University Press, 1988) 205–19. For a more comprehensive and general analysis of the use of Scripture by the New Testament writers, see Klyne Snodgrass, "The Use of the Old Testament in the New," *New Testament Criticism & Interpretation* (Grand Rapids, Mich.: Zondervan Publishing House, 1991) 409–34. For an analysis of the phenomenon in the context of the broader Jewish use of Scripture in the late Second Temple period, see Jacob Neusner, *What Is Midrash?* (Philadelphia: Fortress Press, 1987); and Joseph A. Fitzmyer, "The Use of Explicit Old Testament Quotations in Qumran Literature and in the New Testament," *New Testament Studies* 7/4 (July 1961) 297–333.

[3] For a nice overview of the history of biblical interpretation, see Robert M. Grant with David Tracy, *A Short History of the Interpretation of the Bible,* 2nd ed. (Philadelphia: Fortress Press, 1984). For discussions of current hermeneutical debates, see

issue that has been the subject of serious disagreement, especially among Protestants, is the degree to which Old Testament injunctions should be applied in the life of the Church and the Christian.[4] Are Christians obligated to obey "Old Testament" commands? Different answers to this question have contributed to the rise of the various Protestant theological systems and denominations. Reformed (Calvinist) scholars argue for as much continuity between biblical epochs as possible and, in keeping with this conviction, argue for the relevance of the Law for Christians.[5] Dispensationalists, on the other hand, tend to emphasize discontinuity between the Old and the New, focusing on the newness of the event of Christ. The Dispensationalists, who have greatly influenced large numbers of American Protestants, even extend this discontinuity into the interpretation of certain New Testament writings. Some argue, for example, that significant portions of Jesus' instruction in the Synoptic Gospels do not apply to the Christian in this "age of the Church" but are, rather, intended for a future millennial reign of Christ.[6]

The inclusion of the pre-Christian Scriptures in the catholic biblical canon, supported and strengthened by the canonization of Acts, has mandated the use of those Scriptures in some way by the Church. Nevertheless, many differences and unanswered questions remain in regard to issues of interpretation and relevance.

Moises Silva, *Has the Church Misread the Bible? The History of Interpretation in the Light of Current Issues* (Grand Rapids, Mich.: Zondervan Publishing House, 1987); and Grant R. Osborne, *The Hermeneutical Spiral: A Comprehensive Introduction to Biblical Interpretation* (Downers Grove, Ill.: InterVarsity Press, 1991).

[4] As Schneiders notes in discussing the use of the Old Testament by the early Christians, "the recognition that an ancient document is no longer assimilable purely on face value but that it is too significant to be abandoned as irrelevant or assigned merely historical interest" lies at the heart of the hermeneutical question. She identifies the "actualizing of the perennial value of the classical text" as the central task of interpretation. My point here is that the question remains a live one within the Christian community to this day. See Sandra M. Schneiders, "Scripture and Spirituality," *Christian Spirituality: Origins to the Twelfth Century,* ed. B. McGinn and J. Meyendorff (New York: Crossroad, 1985) 8.

[5] This does not include the ceremonial laws of the Torah, which are believed to have been abrogated with the establishment of the new covenant "in [Christ's] blood" (Luke 22:20).

[6] See, for example, the discussion in Vern S. Poythress, *Understanding Dispensationalists,* 2nd ed. (Phillipsburg: Presbyterian and Reformed Publishing Co., 1994) 30–38. Some portions are also limited to the original followers of Jesus before Pentecost according to this view.

Ecclesiastical Authority

The Church fathers who recognized the value and authority of Acts saw support in the text for their claims of apostolic succession. This issue has divided Western Christianity since the time of the Reformation. Does Acts support the claim of Eastern Orthodox, Roman Catholic, and Anglican leaders that the bishops of the Church are the legitimate successors of the apostles and guardians of the faith? It seems to me that Acts allows for such a claim without specifically endorsing it. The Ephesian paradigm documented in Acts 18–20 establishes a close connection between an apostle, the Holy Spirit, and the overseers of the Ephesian church, but the text falls short of claiming *apostolic* appointment of the overseers. According to the text, the Holy Spirit is given to the Ephesians through the ministry of Paul, and that same Spirit appoints overseers, but the text does not claim that Paul himself chose or appointed those *"episcopous."* It seems to me that those groups of Christians who do not claim apostolic succession in the strict historical sense can justify their ecclesiology on the basis of Acts as long as there is recognizable continuity with the early catholic Christians in their interpretation of the New Testament.[7]

Unity and Diversity

What can the study of the canonical function of Acts contribute to the thorny problem of the unity and diversity of the biblical canon and of Christianity itself? It would seem that the canonization of Acts confirms the importance of the issue and may provide general guidelines for its resolution. The diversity of the texts found within the Bible—texts implicitly endorsed by the presence of Acts in the canon—would seem to legitimize a measure of diversity within the community that canonized those texts and which continues to affirm their canonicity, namely, the various manifestations of catholic Christianity today.[8] On the other hand, the canonization of Acts would seem to reinforce the need for all of the canonical voices to be heard and somehow incorporated into the consciousness of the Church. As Sanders observes, "The pluralism of the [Bible] . . . provides it with its own built-in self-corrective apparatus so

---

[7] Of course, any case for the legitimacy of the apostolic succession today would have to be based on more than the apostolic appointment of elders in the first century.

[8] As is the case throughout this project, I use the phrase "catholic Christianity" to refer to that form of Christianity which developed gradually throughout the early history of the Church and which today manifests itself in Eastern Orthodoxy, Roman Catholicism, and Protestantism.

that we do not absolutize the parts we like and ignore those that challenge our views. . . ."[9]

The problem here is that the catholic authority structure, composed of diverse canonical documents, a unifying element (Acts), and a hermeneutical claim (with an apparent basis in Acts), is faced with a problem that Marcion with his canon probably avoided: the tendency to engage in artificial harmonization. This phenomenon stems from the canonization of diverse documents that are used to support one particular theological system. The irony of this lies in the nature of catholicism (universalism) itself. Catholicism by its very nature incorporates a diversity of voices both historically and geographically. It insists on the inclusion in its biblical canon of both the rational wisdom of Proverbs and the supra-rational wisdom of Job, the Deuteronomistic history and that of the Chronicler, the inclusiveness of Ruth and the exclusiveness of Ezra-Nehemiah, the Synoptic Gospels and the Gospel of John, and the epistles of both Paul and James. Furthermore, it argues that its doctrines were formulated on the basis of (patristic) witnesses from churches in a number of geographical areas, including Palestine, Asia Minor, Rome, Gaul, North Africa, and Egypt. All of this represents the catholic conviction that religious doctrine is not the creation of any one individual or church. Yet throughout its early and later history, catholicism consistently engaged in the denunciation of diversity of perspective and did not hesitate to condemn dissenters to human and/or divine judgment. This appears to have stemmed from the catholic conviction that truth is a unity, from the failure of the Church to distinguish between what is central and what is not, and from the lack of distinction between truth and the interpretation of truth. This tension between unity and diversity clearly surfaced with the Protestant Reformation of the sixteenth century and continued to manifest itself with the rise of the multitude of Protestant denominations in the centuries that followed, each of which has been able to defend its own theological system and ecclesiastical structure on the basis of the biblical canon.

Is a greater tolerance of diversity of interpretation within the unity of the Church possible without abandoning the theological achievements and pronouncements of the canonizing (patristic) community? It seems to me that there is an unrealized potential within Christianity for such a tolerance within certain boundaries. Even the fierce polemicist Tertullian acknowledged the presence and legitimacy of a limited diversity within the Christian tradition when in the context of a discussion of the various biblical texts he penned the following words:

[9] James Sanders, *From Sacred Story to Sacred Text: Canon as Paradigm* (Philadelphia: Fortress Press, 1987) 7.

I do not deny that there is a difference in the language of their documents, in their precepts of virtue, and in their teachings of the law; but yet all this diversity is consistent with one and the same God, even Him by whom it was arranged and also foretold (*Adv. Marc.* 4.1).

Augustine, whose principles of biblical exegesis greatly influenced the Church's reading of Scripture for centuries to come, and whose manual *On Christian Doctrine* was the "Magna Carta of the biblical culture of the Middle Ages,"[10] once asked,

[Since] I believe in [the two great commandments of loving God and humanity] . . . how can it harm me that it should be possible to interpret these words [of Scripture] in several ways, all of which may yet be true? How can it harm me if I understand the writer's meaning in a different sense from that in which another understands it. . . . [What] harm is there if a reader believes what you, the Light of all truthful minds, show him to be the true meaning? It may not even be the meaning which the writer had in mind, and yet he too saw in them a true meaning, different though it may have been from this.[11]

Is there not a principle here that needs to be applied today? The Bible both affirms diversity and provides examples of its limitation, and its structure demands further reflection on how the issue of unity and diversity should be resolved both within the Church and between the Church and those communities outside it with whom it shares common ground. The patristic use of Acts partially explains how the Church could accept and promote a diverse group of texts as a unified corpus. Can it be that by uniting the canonical authorities pneumatologically Luke has unwittingly sanctioned diversity? It may be that the patristic use of Acts can be expanded in the contemporary world to include and sanction the real diversity that exists in the Bible and which has always existed within Christianity. Wall and Lemcio argue that the diversity of the biblical canon functions as a "self-correcting and mutually informing" phenomenon and that the variety of biblical voices should remain in dialectical tension rather than synthesized into one theological system; for to do the latter would be to "de-canonize" the texts of Scripture.[12] This "conversational" understanding of the biblical voices provides

[10] Schneiders, "Scripture and Spirituality," 14.

[11] *Confessions* 12.18 in Saint Augustine, *Confessions*, trans. R. S. Pine-Coffin (London: Penguin Books, 1961).

[12] R. W. Wall and E. E. Lemcio, *The New Testament as Canon: A Reader in Canonical Criticism* (Sheffield: JSOT Press, 1992) 20–21.

one alternative for those who value all the biblical texts associated with the authorities legitimized by the Acts of the Apostles and who also recognize the diversity of the Bible.

There is another major alternative for those who recognize both the authority and the diversity of the biblical texts, as well as the diversity of Christianity itself: the concept of the "canon within the canon." This issue is a live one within the field of canonical criticism. For example, Childs, Gamble, Metzger, and Dunn all include in their works discussions of the issue of levels of authority within the Bible.[13] The question is virtually unavoidable today for two primary reasons. First, as Gamble observes, the modern recognition of the diversity of the Bible virtually forces the interpreter to ask the question of levels of authority within Scripture.[14] Second, as Dunn notes, we must recognize the historical fact that no Christian church or group has ever treated the New Testament writings as uniformly canonical. He is correct in asserting that "[whatever] the theory of canonicity, the reality is that all Christians have operated with a canon within the canon."[15] It would seem that the canonization of Acts within Christianity has reinforced the authoritative nature of *all* the sections of Bible, but is this authority necessarily uniform? More research on the potential for Acts to justify a "canon within the canon" and to provide guidelines for such a notion needs to be undertaken by New Testament scholars. Here I merely offer two observations from Acts 15 as suggestive of the potential of Acts in this regard.

The first observation comes from the decision of the council regarding the Gentiles and the Law of Moses. According to the text, the apostles decided that the Gentiles were not bound to the Mosaic Covenant. This, of course, has been the enduring position of catholic Christianity, largely under the influence of Pauline thought. And yet the Torah is included in the catholic canon. How can Torah be "authoritative" over Gentile Christians and nonbinding at the same time? It seems

---

[13] Brevard S. Childs, *The New Testament as Canon: An Introduction*, 2nd ed. (Valley Forge, Pa.: Trinity Press International, 1994) 20; Harry Y. Gamble, *The New Testament Canon: Its Making and Meaning* (Philadelphia: Fortress Press, 1985) 86–89; Bruce M. Metzger, *The Canon of the New Testament: Its Origin, Development, and Significance* (Oxford: Oxford University Press, 1987) 275–82; James D. G. Dunn, *Unity and Diversity in the New Testament: An Inquiry into the Character of Earliest Christianity*, 2nd ed. (Philadelphia: Trinity Press International, 1990) 374–76.

[14] Gamble, *NT Canon*, 85–86.

[15] Dunn, *Unity and Diversity*, 374. Dunn provides a number of examples which illustrate his point, including the traditional Roman Catholic propensity to rely heavily on Matthew and the Pastoral epistles, the Eastern Orthodox use of the Johannine Writings, and the Protestant appeal to particular Pauline letters.

to me that we have here a fascinating and unique phenomenon within the history of the Western religions in general and the history of the biblical canon in particular: A collection of texts canonized in one community for one primary purpose has been recognized by another community as canonical for a different purpose.[16] The Torah originally functioned (and to a certain extent continues to function) in Judaism as a *legally* authoritative corpus, whereas in Christianity it appears to function primarily as a *theologically* authoritative one; that is, as an authoritative foreshadowing of the atoning work of Christ. For the catholics who recognized its canonicity, the Old Testament taken as a whole predicted both the coming of Christ and the outpouring of the Holy Spirit on the Church. According to Acts 15, it was the coming of the Spirit on Gentile believers that led the apostles to conclude that the Law was not binding upon these believers, an event that contributed to this change in the way Torah was viewed. In this case, it is this event that seems to provide the "canon" by which the Scriptures are interpreted and applied in the community. The principle of the "canon within the canon" appears to find some support here in that the work of the Spirit in the Gentile believers made their subjection to the injunctions of the Torah unnecessary in the judgment of the apostles. Since this has been the enduring perspective of Christianity, is it not possible that the New Testament texts which describe the work of the Spirit in the Church do and/or should function as part of a "canon within the canon"?

A second observation from Acts 15 may also support this notion. In Luke's account of the council, James quotes Amos 9:11-12 in reference to the coming of the Spirit on the Gentiles, an event which Peter describes. James then asserts that "the words of the prophets are in agreement with this" (NIV).[17] As Johnson notes, what is remarkable about this is the way in which James links the Scripture with the experience of the Gentiles. He does not say that their experience agrees with the Scripture, but that the Scripture agrees with their experience, implying that the latter serves as the basis for interpreting the former.[18] At a minimum this would seem to underscore the authority of the more recent biblical revelations over earlier ones. Of course, any notion of a hierarchy

---

[16] This seems to be more than just one manifestation of the various reader-oriented (midrashic) interpretations of Scripture current in first-century Judaism. Here, Torah is not being applied to the daily practices of the community; the community is distancing itself from the particular requirements of the text *and* recognizing its canonicity at the same time.

[17] *toutō sumphōnousin hoi logoi tōn prophētōn*

[18] Johnson, *Acts*, 271.

of authority within Scripture would have to preserve the integrity of *all* the biblical texts if Acts is to be used as its basis. Suggestions like that of Harnack, for example, that the Old Testament be removed from the canon, would not be acceptable.

Whether one views the canon as a collection of equally authoritative but diverse voices in conversation with one another, or as a collection of texts containing a hierarchy of authoritative texts and teachings, the presence of Acts within the canon (with its sanctioning of each of the major sections of the Bible) would seem to underscore the need for particular portions of Scripture to correct Christians who want to lean only on those texts which seem most clearly to support *their* particular religious preferences, whether in regard to belief or practice. At the same time, however, it may provide guidelines for more carefully nuanced understandings of the authority of a diverse canon by providing guidelines for the establishment of a "canon" within the biblical canon. Either or both alternatives to the traditional understanding of a uniformly authoritative Bible may help the Christian community to gain a better understanding of its sacred texts and to resolve the issues raised by diverse interpretations of that text in the contemporary Church.

Contemporary Canon Studies

Most of the research into the formation of the biblical canon undertaken by scholars over the past half century or so has attempted to deal with the development of either the Old or New Testament canon as a whole. We currently have partial answers to the general questions associated with these processes. For example, scholars have addressed the questions of why the Church felt the need to have any canon at all, why it took the time that it did for the final shape of the canon to become clear, and what general factors contributed to the formation of that canon. But questions remain as to why particular texts were included and others excluded. I have argued that the book of Acts was canonized because it had particular value for the canonizing community. It is reasonable to assume that other texts were also canonized for the value of their content. More research needs to be done into the canonization of other texts with the value principle as the operative guideline. Questions regarding the canonization of particular texts may be answered through research into the specific use of those texts in the ancient Jewish and Christian communities.

References to the Holy Spirit in Acts

1:2   Jesus gives commands to the apostles through the HS

1:5   Jesus promises the baptism of the HS to the apostles

1:8   Baptism of HS will result in power to testify everywhere

1:16   The HS had predicted through David the ruin of Judas

2:4a   Apostles (disciples?) receive (are filled with) the HS during Pentecost

2:4b   The HS causes the apostles (disciples?) to speak in tongues

2:17   Joel had predicted the outpouring of the HS "in the last days"

2:18   Joel had predicted that the HS would cause men and women to prophesy

2:33   Peter credits Jesus with the outpouring of the HS

2:38   Peter offers the HS (and forgiveness) to his Jewish listeners on the condition of repentance and baptism

4:8   Peter, filled with the HS, defends himself before the Jewish leaders in Jerusalem

4:25?   The apostles (disciples?) worship God at the release of Peter and John, and credit God with having spoken by the HS through David in Psalm 2 (textual variant)

4:31   The apostles (disciples?) pray for boldness, are filled with the HS, and speak the word of God with boldness

5:3   Peter accuses Ananias of lying to the HS

5:9   Peter accuses Sapphira (and Ananias posthumously) of testing the HS

5:32   The apostles defend themselves before the Jewish leaders in Jerusalem by claiming to be co-witnesses with the HS of Jesus' resurrection, exaltation, and offer of repentance and forgiveness of sin to Israel

6:3   The apostles identify the filling of the HS as one of the requirements of the seven table-servers

6:5   Stephen, one of the seven, is a man full of faith and the HS

6:10?   Stephen's accusers are unable to resist the wisdom and the spirit/Spirit by which he speaks

7:51   Stephen accuses the Jewish leaders in Jerusalem of always resisting the HS

7:55   Stephen is filled with the HS during his trial and has a vision of Jesus

8:15   Peter and John go to Samaria to pray for the Samaritans' reception of the HS (for those who "had only been baptized in the name of the Lord Jesus")

8:17   Peter and John lay hands on the Samaritans and they receive the HS

8:18   Simon the sorcerer witnesses the apostles' ability to give the HS by the laying on of hands

8:19   Simon the sorcerer offers money and requests from the apostles the ability to give the HS

8:29   The HS instructs Philip to overtake the chariot of the Ethiopian eunuch

8:39   The HS "catches Philip away" after the Ethiopian's baptism

9:17   Ananias, a Damascus disciple, lays hands on Paul to restore Paul's sight and cause him to be filled with the HS

9:31   Believers in Judea, Galilee, and Samaria experience the comfort of the HS after Paul's conversion

10:19   The HS instructs Peter to go with the messengers of Cornelius

10:38   Peter tells Cornelius that Jesus had been anointed with the HS and with power by God

10:44   The HS falls on Cornelius and those with him during Peter's sermon

10:45   The Jewish Christians with Peter are astonished that the HS had been "poured out on the Gentiles also"

10:47   Peter reasons that these Gentile believers should be baptized because they have received the HS, and he commands them to be baptized

11:12   Peter defends himself to Jewish believers in Jerusalem by explaining that the HS had instructed him to go to the Gentile Cornelius's house

11:15   Peter explains that the HS fell on these Gentiles during his sermon

11:16 Peter explains that when the HS fell on the Gentiles he remembered Jesus' prediction of the baptism of the HS

11:24 Barnabas is sent out by the Jerusalem church to investigate the conversion of Hellenists in Antioch; he is "full of the HS"

11:28 Agabus, a prophet from Jerusalem, prophesies in Antioch through the HS concerning the great famine to come

13:2 The HS instructs the leaders in Antioch to appoint Barnabas and Paul as missionaries

13:4 After the leaders lay hands on Barnabas and Paul, Luke claims that the HS sent them out

13:9 Paul, full of the HS, rebukes and blinds a sorcerer who seeks to thwart the evangelization of the proconsul in Salamis

13:52 The disciples in Pisidia are full of joy and the HS, in spite of persecution against Paul and Barnabas

15:8 Peter defends the Gentile mission by arguing that God had demonstrated His acceptance of the Gentiles apart from the Mosaic law by giving them the HS

15:28 James declares that it seemed good to both the HS and the council participants to side against the Christian Pharisees

16:6 The HS forbids Paul and company to preach in Asia

16:7 The HS forbids Paul and company to go into Bithynia

18:5? Textual variant: Paul was either "occupied with the word" or "constrained by the Spirit/spirit" in his preaching at Corinth

19:2a Paul asks some disciples of John the Baptist if they had received the HS when they believed

19:2b These disciples respond that they have not even heard of the HS (or about the giving of the HS)

19:6 After these disciples are baptized in the name of Jesus, Paul lays hands on them and they receive the HS

19:21? Paul purposes in/by the spirit/Spirit to go to Jerusalem and then to Rome

20:22? Paul explains that he is going to Jerusalem bound in/with/by/to the spirit/Spirit

20:23 Paul declares that the HS has been testifying in every city that tribulation awaits him

20:28 Paul reminds the Ephesian elders that the HS had made them "bishops" over the church

21:4   Disciples at Tyre warn Paul through the HS not to go up to Jerusalem

21:11   Agabus predicts by the HS that Paul will be arrested in Jerusalem

28:25   Paul declares that the HS had spoken rightly through the prophet Isaiah concerning Israel

Bibliography

Achtemeier, Paul J. *The Quest for Unity in the New Testament Church.* Philadelphia: Fortress Press, 1987.

Aland, B., K. Aland, J. Karavidopoulos, C. Martini, and B. Metier, eds. *The Greek New Testament.* 4th rev. ed. D-Stuttgart: Deutsche Bibelgesellschaft, 1994.

Aland, Kurt. *The Problem of the New Testament Canon.* London: A. R. Mowbray & Co. Ltd., 1962.

Augustine. *Confessions.* Trans. R. S. Pine-Coffin. London: Penguin Books, 1961.

Aune, David E. *Prophecy in Early Christianity and the Ancient Mediterranean World.* Grand Rapids, Mich.: William B. Eerdmans Publishing Co., 1983.

Balas, David L. "Marcion Revisited: A 'Post-Harnack' Perspective." *Texts and Testaments: Critical Essays on the Bible and Early Church Fathers.* Ed. W. E. March, 95–108. San Antonio: Trinity University Press, 1980.

Barr, James. *Holy Scripture: Canon, Authority, Criticism.* Oxford: Oxford University Press, 1983.

Barrett, C. K. "Paul and the 'Pillar' Apostles." *Studia Paulina.* Haarlem: De Erven F. Bohn N.V., 1953.

Barton, John. *Reading the Old Testament: Method in Biblical Study.* 2nd ed. London: Darton, Longman and Todd Ltd., 1996.

Baxter, Margaret. *The Formation of the Christian Scriptures.* Philadelphia: The Westminster Press, 1988.

Beckwith, Roger. *The Old Testament Canon of the New Testament Church and Its Background in Early Judaism.* London: SPCK, 1985.

Bede, the Venerable. *Commentary on the Acts of the Apostles.* Trans. L. T. Martin. Kalamazoo, Mich.: Cistercian Publications, 1989.

_____. *The Commentary on the Seven Catholic Epistles of Bede the Venerable.* Trans. D. Hurst. Kalamazoo, Mich.: Cistercian Publications, 1985.

Bovon, François. *New Testament Traditions and Apocryphal Narratives.* Trans. Jane Haapisera-Hunter. Allison Park: Pickwick Publications, 1995.

_____. "The Synoptic Gospels and the Noncanonical Acts of the Apostles." *Harvard Theological Review* 81/1 (1988) 19–36.

Brehm, H. Alan. "Paul's Relationship with the Jerusalem Apostles in Galatians 1 and 2." *Southwestern Journal of Theology* 37/1 (Fall 1994) 11–16.

Brenneman, James E. *Canons in Conflict: Negotiating Texts in True and False Prophecy.* New York: Oxford University Press, 1997.

Brooks, James A. "The Place of James in the New Testament Canon." *Southwestern Journal of Theology* 12/1 (Fall 1969) 41–55.

Brown, Schuyler. "Apostleship in the New Testament as an Historical and Theological Problem." *New Testament Studies* 30 (1984) 474–80.

Brown, S. K. "James: A Religio-Historical Study of the Relations between Jewish, Gnostic, and Catholic Christianity in the Earliest Period through an Investigation of the Traditions about James the Lord's Brother." Ph.D. Dissertation, Brown University, 1972.

Bruce, F. F. *The Canon of Scripture.* Downers Grove, Ill.: InterVarsity Press, 1988.

_____. *The Book of Acts.* Revised ed. Grand Rapids, Mich.: William B. Eerdmans Publishing Co., 1988.

_____. "The Holy Spirit in the Acts of the Apostles." *Interpretation: A Journal of Bible and Theology* 27/2 (April 1973) 166–83.

Campenhausen, Hans von. *Ecclesiastical Authority and Spiritual Power in the Church of the First Three Centuries.* Trans. J. A. Baker. Stanford: Stanford University Press, 1969.

_____. *The Formation of the Christian Bible.* Trans. J. A. Baker. Philadelphia: Fortress Press, 1972.

Carroll, John T. "The Uses of Scripture in Acts." *Society of Biblical Literature 1990 Seminar Papers* 29 (1990) 512–28.

Carroll, Kenneth L. "The Place of James in the Early Church." *Bulletin of the John Rylands Library* 44 (1961–62) 49–67.

Catchpole, David R. "Paul, James and the Apostolic Decree." *New Testament Studies* 23/4 (July 1977) 428–44.

Childs, Brevard S. *The New Testament as Canon: An Introduction.* 2nd ed. Valley Forge, Pa.: Trinity Press International, 1994.

Clabeaux, John J. *A Lost Edition of the Letters of Paul: A Reassessment of the Text of the Pauline Corpus Attested by Marcion.* Washington, D.C.: The Catholic Biblical Association of America, 1989.

Cohen, Shaye J. D. "The Significance of Yavneh: Pharisees, Rabbis, and the End of Jewish Sectarianism." *Hebrew Union College Annual* 55 (1984) 27–53.

Comfort, Philip W., ed. *The Origin of the Bible.* Wheaton: Tyndale House Publishers, Inc., 1992.

Coward, Harold. *Sacred Word and Sacred Text: Scripture in World Religions.* Maryknoll, N.Y.: Orbis Books, 1988.

Darr, John A. "Spirit and Power in Luke-Acts." An unpublished paper presented at the annual meeting of the Society of Biblical Literature, San Francisco, Calif., November 22, 1997.

Denny, Frederick M., and Rodney L. Taylor, eds. *The Holy Book in Comparative Perspective.* Columbia: University of South Carolina Press, 1985.

Desjardins, Michel. "Introduction to VII,3: Apocalypse of Peter." *The Coptic Gnostic Library: Nag Hammadi Codex VII.* Ed. B. Pearson, 201–47. Leiden: E. J. Brill, 1996.

Dunbar, D. G., R. B. Gaffin Jr., K. Kantzer, D. G. Meade, K. Snodgrass, and R. Youngblood. "The Canon: How God Gave His Word to the Church." *Christianity Today* (February 5, 1988) 23–38.

Dunn, James D. G. *Unity and Diversity in the New Testament: An Inquiry into the Character of Earliest Christianity.* Revised ed. Philadelphia: Trinity Press International, 1990.

Dupont, Jacques. "The Use of the Old Testament in the Acts." *Theology Digest* 3 (1955) 61–64.

Ehrman, Bart D. *The Orthodox Corruption of Scripture.* New York: Oxford University Press, 1993.

Elliott, J. K. *The Apocryphal New Testament.* New York: Oxford University Press, 1993.

Epiphanius. *The Panarion.* Book 1. Trans. Frank Williams. Leiden: E. J. Brill, 1987.

Farmer, W. R., and D. M. Farkasfalvy. *The Formation of the New Testament Canon: An Ecumenical Approach.* New York: Paulist Press, 1983.

Ferguson, E. "Canon Muratori: Date and Provenance." *Studia Patristica* 17 (1982) 677–83.

Fitzmyer, Joseph A. "The Use of Explicit Old Testament Quotations in Qumran Literature and in the New Testament." *New Testament Studies* 7/4 (July 1961) 297–333.

Florovsky, Georges. *Bible, Church, Tradition: An Eastern Orthodox View.* Belmont: Nordland Publishing Co., 1972.

Freedman, David N. "How the Hebrew Bible & the Christian Old Testament Differ: Interview with David N. Freedman, Part One." Interviewed by Hershel Shanks. *Bible Review* (December 1993) 28–39.

_____. "The Undiscovered Symmetry of the Bible: Interview with David N. Freedman, Part Two." Interviewed by Hershel Shanks. *Bible Review* (February 1994) 34–40.

Frend, W.H.C. *The Early Church: From the Beginnings to 461.* 3rd ed. London: SCM Press, Ltd., 1991.

Frye, Northrop. *Words with Power: Being a Second Study of "The Bible and Literature."* San Diego: Harcourt Brace Jovanovich, Publishers, 1990.

Gallagher, Eugene V. "Conversion and Salvation in the Apocryphal Acts of the Apostles." *The Second Century: A Journal of Early Christian Studies* 8/1 (Spring 1991) 13–29.

Gamble, Harry Y. *The New Testament Canon: Its Making and Meaning.* Philadelphia: Fortress Press, 1985.

Goulder, Michael D. "Did Luke Know Any of the Pauline Letters?" *Perspectives in Religious Studies* 13/2 (Summer 1986) 97–112.

Grant, Robert M. *The Formation of the New Testament.* New York: Harper & Row, 1965.

_____. "Gnostic Spirituality." *Christian Spirituality: Origins to the Twelfth Century.* Ed. B. McGinn and J. Meyendorff, 44–60. New York: Crossroad, 1985.

_____. "Marcion and the Critical Method." *From Jesus to Paul: Studies in Honour of Francis Wright Beare.* Ed. P. Richardson and J. Hurd, 207–15. Waterloo: Wilfrid Laurier University Press, 1984.

Grant, Robert M., with David Tracy. *A Short History of the Interpretation of the Bible,* 2nd ed. Philadelphia: Fortress Press, 1984.

Greenwald, Michael R. "The New Testament Canon and the Mishnah as Consolidation of Knowledge in the Second Century C.E." *Society of Biblical Literature 1987 Seminar Papers* 26 (1987) 244–54.

Groothuis, Douglas. "The New Testament Canon Faces the New Age Challenge." *Epiphany: A Journal of Faith and Insight* 11/2 (Winter 1991) 17–20.

Grove, Ron. "Canon and Community: Authority in the History of Religions." Ph.D. dissertation, University of California, Santa Barbara, 1983.

Haenchen, Ernst. *The Acts of the Apostles: A Commentary.* Philadelphia: The Westminster Press, 1971.

Harm, Frederick R. "Structural Elements Related to the Gift of the Holy Spirit in Acts." *Concordia Journal* 14/1 (January 1988) 28–41.

The HarperCollins Study Bible: New Revised Standard Version. New York: HarperCollins Publishers, 1993.

Harnack, Adolf von. *The Acts of the Apostles.* Trans. J. R. Wilkinson. New York: G. P. Putnam's Sons, 1909.

_____. *Marcion: The Gospel of the Alien God.* Trans. J. E. Steely and L. D. Bierma. Durham: The Labyrinth Press, 1924/1990 reprint.

_____. *The Origin of the New Testament.* Trans. J. R. Wilkinson. New York: The Macmillan Company, 1925.

Heine, Ronald E. *The Montanist Oracles and Testimonia.* Macon: Mercer University Press, 1989.

Hoffmann, R. Joseph. *Marcion: On the Restitution of Christianity: An Essay on the Development of Radical Paulinist Theology in the Second Century.* Chico: Scholars Press, 1984.

The Holy Bible Containing the Old and New Testaments: The New King James Version. Nashville: Thomas Nelson Publishers, 1983.

The Holy Bible: New International Version. Grand Rapids, Mich.: Zondervan, 1978.

Hoover, Roy W. "How the Books of the New Testament Were Chosen." *Bible Review* (April 1993) 44–47.

Jackson, Pamela. "Cyril of Jerusalem's Treatment of Scriptural Texts Concerning the Holy Spirit." *Tradition: Studies in Ancient and Medieval History, Thought, and Religion* 46 (1991) 1–31.

_____. "Cyril of Jerusalem's Use of Scripture in Catechesis." *Theological Studies* 52 (1991) 431–50.

Jervell, Jacob. "The Acts of the Apostles and the History of Early Christianity." *Studia Theologica: Scandinavian Journal of Theology* 37 (1983) 17–32.

_____. *Luke and the People of God: A New Look at Luke-Acts.* Minneapolis: Augsburg Publishing House, 1972.

Johnson, Luke Timothy. *The Acts of the Apostles.* Collegeville: The Liturgical Press, 1992.

_____. "Glossolalia and the Embarrassments of Experience." *The Princeton Seminary Bulletin* 18/2 (1997) 113–34.

_____. *The Letter of James: A New Translation with Introduction and Commentary.* New York: Doubleday, 1995.

Josephus. "The Antiquities of the Jews." *The Works of Josephus,* new updated ed. Trans. William Whiston. N. P.: Hendrickson Publishers, 1995 reprint.

Jung, C. G. *Psychology and Religion*. New Haven, Conn.: Yale University Press, 1938/1966 reprint.

Keener, Craig S. *The IVP Bible Background Commentary: New Testament*. Downers Grove, Ill.: InterVarsity Press, 1993.

Kline, Meredith G. *The Structure of Biblical Authority*. Grand Rapids, Mich.: William B. Eerdmans Publishing Co., 1972.

Kloppenborg, John S. *The Formation of Q: Trajectories in Ancient Wisdom Collections*. Philadelphia: Fortress Press, 1987/1989 reprint.

Koester, Helmut. *Ancient Christian Gospels: Their History and Development*. Philadelphia: Trinity Press International, 1990.

_____. "Apocryphal and Canonical Gospels." *Harvard Theological Review* 73/1–2 (Jan.–Apr. 1980) 105–30.

_____. *Introduction to the New Testament*. Volume One: *History, Culture, and Religion of the Hellenistic Age*. 2nd ed. New York: Walter De Gruyter, 1995.

_____. *Introduction to the New Testament*. Volume Two: *History and Literature of Early Christianity*. Philadelphia: Fortress Press, 1982.

_____. "Writings and the Spirit: Authority and Politics in Ancient Christianity." *Harvard Theological Review* 84/4 (1991) 353–72.

Kuck, David W. "The Use and Canonization of Acts in the Early Church." STM Thesis, Yale University, 1975.

Levenson, Jon D. "The Bible: Unexamined Commitments of Criticism." *First Things: A Monthly Journal of Religion and Public Life* (February 1993) 24–33.

Levering, Miriam. "Introduction: Rethinking Scripture." *Rethinking Scripture: Essays from a Comparative Perspective*. Ed. M. Levering, 1–17. Albany: SUNY Press, 1989.

Levinas, Emmanuel. "The Jewish Understanding of Scripture." Trans. J. Cunneen. *Cross Currents: The Journal of the Association for Religion and Intellectual Life* 44/4 (Winter 1994–95) 488–504.

Liddell and Scott. *An Intermediate Greek-English Lexicon*. Oxford: Oxford University Press, 1889/1994 reprint.

Lightfoot, J. B., and J. R. Harmer, eds. *The Apostolic Fathers: Revised Greek Texts with Introductions and English Translations*. Grand Rapids, Mich.: Baker Book House, 1984 reprint.

Lightstone, Jack N. "Talmudic Rabbinism, Midrash, and the Fragmentation of Scripture." *Society of Biblical Literature Seminar Papers* 25 (1986) 614–30.

Longenecker, Richard N. "The Acts of the Apostles." *The Expositor's Bible Commentary*, Vol. 9. Grand Rapids, Mich.: Zondervan Publishing House, 1981.

Lührmann, Dieter. "Gal. 2:9 und die katholischen Briefe." *Zeitschrift für Die Neutestamentliche Wissenschaft* 72 (1981) 65–87.

Marsh, Thomas. "Holy Spirit in Early Christian Teaching." *The Irish Theological Quarterly* 45/2 (1978) 101–16.

Marshall, I. Howard. "Luke's View of Paul." *Southwestern Journal of Theology* 33/1 (Fall 1990) 41–51.

Martin, Lawrence T. "Bede's Structural Use of Wordplay as a Way to Teach." *From Cloister to Classroom: Monastic and Scholastic Approaches to Truth*, 27–46. Kalamazoo, Mich.: Cistercian Publications, Inc., 1986.

McDonald, Lee Martin. *The Formation of the Christian Biblical Canon*. Nashville: Abingdon Press, 1988.

Meade, David G. *Pseudonymity & Canon: An Investigation into the Relationship of Authorship and Authority in Jewish and Earliest Christian Tradition.* Grand Rapids, Mich.: William B. Eerdmans Publishing Co., 1987.

Metzger, Bruce M. *The Canon of the New Testament: Its Origin, Development, and Significance.* Oxford: Oxford University Press, 1987.

_____. *The Text of the New Testament: Its Transmission, Corruption, and Restoration.* 3rd ed. New York: Oxford University Press, 1992.

Meyer, Marvin W. "NHC VIII,2: The Letter of Peter to Philip: Introduction." *The Coptic Gnostic Library: Nag Hammadi Codex VIII.* Ed J. Sieber. Leiden: E. J. Brill, 1991.

Migne, J. P., ed. *Patrologiae Cursus Completus: Series Graeca.* 162 vols. Paris: Migne, 1857–1866.

_____. *Patrologiae Cursus Completus: Series Latina.* 221 vols. Paris: Migne, 1844–1866.

Miller, Robert J., ed. *The Complete Gospels.* Sonoma: Polebridge Press, 1992.

Munck, J. "Jewish Christianity in Post-Apostolic Times." *New Testament Studies* 6/2 (January 1960) 103–16.

Neusner, Jacob. *What Is Midrash?* Philadelphia: Fortress Press, 1987.

Olsen, Glenn. "Bede as Historian: The Evidence from His Observations on the Life of the First Christian Community at Jerusalem." *Journal of Ecclesiastical History* 33/4 (October 1982) 519–30.

Osborn, Eric F. "Reason and the Rule of Faith in the Second Century AD." *The Making of Orthodoxy.* Ed. R. Williams, 40–61. Cambridge: Cambridge University Press, 1989.

Osborne, Grant R. *The Hermeneutical Spiral: A Comprehensive Introduction to Biblical Interpretation.* Downers Grove, Ill.: InterVarsity Press, 1991.

Outler, Albert C. "The 'Logic' of Canon-making and the Tasks of Canon-criticism." *Texts and Testaments: Critical Essays on the Bible and Early Church Fathers.* Ed. W. E. March, 263–76. San Antonio: Trinity University Press, 1980.

Pagels, Elaine H. "Visions, Appearances, and Apostolic Authority: Gnostic and Orthodox Traditions." *Gnosis: Festschrift für Hans Jonas.* Göttingen: Vandenhoeck & Ruprecht, 1978.

Painchaud, Louis. "The Use of Scripture in Gnostic Literature." *Journal of Early Christian Studies* 4 (1996) 129–46.

Patterson, L. G. "Irenaeus and the Valentinians: The Emergence of a Christian Scriptures." *Studia Patristica* 18 (1989) 189–220.

Pearson, Birger A. "Anti-Heretical Warnings in Codex IX from Nag Hammadi." *Essays on the Nag Hammadi Texts in Honour of Pahor Labib,* 145–54. Nag Hammadi Studies, vol. 6. Leiden: E. J. Brill, 1975.

_____. "Introduction to IX,3: The Testimony of Truth." *Nag Hammadi Codices IX and X,* 101–203. Nag Hammadi Studies, vol. 15. Leiden: E. J. Brill, 1981.

_____. "Nag Hammadi." *The Anchor Bible Dictionary.* Ed. David Noel Freedman. Vol. 4, 982–93. New York: Doubleday, 1992.

Perkins, Pheme. *Gnosticism and the New Testament.* Minneapolis: Fortress Press, 1993.

Person, Ralph E. "The Mode of Theological Decision Making at the Early Ecumenical Councils: An Inquiry into the Function of Scripture and Tradition at the Councils of Nicaea and Ephesus." D.Theol. dissertation, The University of Basel, 1978.

Pervo, Richard I. "Early Christian Fiction." *Greek Fiction: The Greek Novel in Context.* Ed. J. R. Morgan and R. Stoneman, 239–53. New York: Routledge Press, 1994.

_____. *Profit with Delight: The Literary Genre of the Acts of the Apostles.* Philadelphia: Fortress Press, 1987.

Poythress, Vern S. *Understanding Dispensationalists.* 2nd ed. Phillipsburg: Presbyterian and Reformed Publishing Co., 1994.

Praeder, Susan M. "Jesus-Paul, Peter-Paul, and Jesus-Peter Parallelisms in Luke-Acts: A History of Reader Response." *Society of Biblical Literature 1984 Seminar Papers* 23 (1984) 23–39.

Quasten, Johannes. *Patrology.* Volumes 1–3. Westminster: The Newman Press, 1951–1955.

Roberts, A., and J. Donaldson, eds. *Ante-Nicene Christian Library.* Grand Rapids, Mich.: William B. Eerdmans Publishing Co., 1983–1989 reprints.

Robinson, James M. *Nag Hammadi: The First Fifty Years.* Claremont: The Institute for Antiquity and Christianity, 1995.

Rusch, William G., ed. *The Trinitarian Controversy.* Philadelphia: Fortress Press, 1980.

Sanders, Jack T. "The Prophetic Use of the Scriptures in Luke-Acts." *Early Jewish and Christian Exegesis.* Ed. Craig A. Evans and William F. Stinespring. 191–98. Atlanta: Scholars Press, 1987.

Sanders, James A. *Canon and Community: A Guide to Canonical Criticism.* Philadelphia: Fortress Press, 1984.

_____. *From Sacred Story to Sacred Text.* Philadelphia: Fortress Press, 1987.

_____. *Torah and Canon.* Philadelphia: Fortress Press, 1972.

Schaff, P., ed. *A Select Library of Nicene and Post-Nicene Fathers of the Christian Church,* First Series. Grand Rapids, Mich.: William B. Eerdmans Publishing Co., 1983–1989 reprints.

Schaff, P., and H. Wace, eds. *A Select Library of Nicene and Post-Nicene Fathers of the Christian Church,* Second Series. Grand Rapids, Mich.: William B. Eerdmans Publishing Co., 1983–1989 reprints.

Schneiders, Sandra M. "Scripture and Spirituality." *Christian Spirituality: Origins to the Twelfth Century.* Ed. B. McGinn and J. Meyendorff, 1–20. New York: Crossroad, 1985.

Short, Augustus. *The Witness of the Spirit with Our Spirit.* London: J. H. Parker, F. and J. Rivington, 1846.

Silva, Moises. *Has the Church Misread the Bible? The History of Interpretation in the Light of Current Issues.* Grand Rapids, Mich.: Zondervan Publishing House, 1987.

Sloan, Robert B. "Unity in Diversity: A Clue to the Emergence of the New Testament as Sacred Literature." *New Testament Criticism & Interpretation.* Ed. D. A. Black and D. S. Dockery, 437–68. Grand Rapids, Mich.: Zondervan Publishing House, 1991.

Smith, M. "The Reason for the Persecution of Paul and the Obscurity of Acts." *Studies in Mysticism and Religion,* 261–68. Jerusalem: The Hebrew University, 1967.

Smith, Wilfred Cantwell. *What Is Scripture? A Comparative Approach.* Minneapolis: Fortress Press, 1993.

Snodgrass, Klyne. "The Use of the Old Testament in the New." *New Testament Criticism & Interpretation.* Ed. D. Black and D. Dockery, 409–34. Grand Rapids, Mich.: Zondervan Publishing House, 1991.

Soards, Marion L. *The Speeches in Acts: Their Content, Context, and Concerns.* Louisville: Westminster/John Knox Press, 1994.

Sommer, Benjamin D. "Did Prophecy Cease? Evaluating a Reevaluation." *Journal of Biblical Literature* 115/1 (Spring 1996) 31–47.

Stanton, Graham. "Matthew." *It Is Written: Scripture Citing Scripture.* Ed. D. Carson and H. Williamson, 205–19. New York: Cambridge University Press, 1988.

Stowers, Stanley K. *A Rereading of Romans: Justice, Jews, and Gentiles.* New Haven, Conn.: Yale University Press, 1994.

Sundberg, Albert C., Jr. "Canon Muratori: A Fourth-Century List." *Harvard Theological Review* 66/1 (January 1973) 1–41.

_____. "Towards a Revised History of the New Testament Canon." *Studia Evangelica* 4 (1968) 452–61.

Thielman, Frank. "The New Testament: Its Basis for Authority." *Westminster Theological Journal* 45/2 (1983) 400–10.

Tilley, Maureen A. "Typological Numbers: Taking a Count of the Bible." *Bible Review* (June 1992) 48–49.

Torrance, Thomas F. "Kerygmatic Proclamation of the Gospel: The Demonstration of Apostolic Preaching of Irenaios of Lyons." *The Greek Orthodox Theological Review* 37/1–2 (1992) 105–21.

VanderKam, James C. *The Dead Sea Scrolls Today.* Grand Rapids, Mich.: William B. Eerdmans Publishing Co., 1994.

Wall, Robert W., and Eugene E. Lemcio. *The New Testament as Canon: A Reader in Canonical Criticism.* Sheffield: JSOT Press, 1992.

Wilken, Robert L. "Marcion" and "Marcionism." *The Encyclopedia of Religion.* Vol. 9. Ed. Mircea Eliade, 194–96. New York: MacMillan Publishing Co., 1987.

Williams, Daniel H. "Harnack, Marcion and the Argument of Antiquity." *Hellenization Revisited: Shaping a Christian Response within the Greco-Roman World.* Ed. Wendy E. Helleman, 223–40. Lanham, Md.: University Press of America, 1994.

Williams, David S. "Reconsidering Marcion's Gospel." *Journal of Biblical Literature* 108/3 (1989) 477–96.

Williams, Michael Allen. *Rethinking "Gnosticism": An Argument for Dismantling a Dubious Category.* Princeton, Ill.: Princeton University Press, 1996.

Wright, Robert B. "Comparative Religious Scripture." Unpublished Paper, September 1996. Temple University, Philadelphia, Pennsylvania.

Wylie, Amanda Berry. "The Exegesis of History in John Chrysostom's *Homilies on Acts.*" *Biblical Hermeneutics in Historical Perspective.* Ed. M. Burrows and P. Rorem, 59–72. Grand Rapids, Mich.: Williamm B. Eerdmans Publishing Co., 1991.